the *Art* of HAND APPLIQUÉ

**PRECISION TECHNIQUES FOR
STITCHING AND PATTERN DRAFTING**

Front cover quilt:

AND CROWN HER GOOD WITH BROTHERHOOD (detail)
72" x 72"
Laura Lee Fritz, 1986.

This quilt took nine months of steady work, twelve and fifteen hours each day. Its characters are of all races and all ages, engaged in activities which bring them closest to their feelings of freedom. The black and white profile silhouettes between the color blocks are caricatures of our forerunners, and a harkening back to the paper-cutting art form of our past.

This hand appliquéd quilt is hand embroidered with single-strand threads and hand quilted.

Full quilt is shown on page 72.

Photographs by Laura Lee Fritz and Ron Paul.

the *Art* of HAND APPLIQUÉ

PRECISION TECHNIQUES FOR STITCHING AND PATTERN DRAFTING

LAURA LEE FRITZ

American Quilter's Society
P.O. Box 3290
Paducah, KY 42002-3290

Table of Contents

Acknowledgments

Special thanks are due:

Jim Fritz for his months of darkroom work to produce the photographs herein,

Ron and Spencer Paul for understanding my drive and supporting me with cheerful spirits,

Marti Fritz for teaching me to love sewing.

Introduction

Appliqué, in its simplest form, is the act of securing one thing to another. This could be by glueing layers of paper or wood together, sewing beads and sequins to cloth, or melting bits of plastic to one another.

A quilter speaking of appliqué means sewing one piece of fabric to another. Machine appliqué done with satin stitches zigzagged over raw edges is popular, and the results can be quite artistic. Hand appliqué can be done with embroidery stitches to decorate turned edges, or with minute stitches invisibly holding the appliqué layer to the base fabric.

This book demonstrates how to achieve fine, invisible hand appliqué – how to use simple basic stitches to achieve effective results. The *dent transfer* technique and *assembly of units* method are two unique processes introduced, and *drafting under-layer flaps for pattern pieces* is another important technique presented.

Each process is explained, illustrated, and practiced to gradually develop skills. Durability, an important concern in appliqué, is a goal throughout, whether the project is simple or complex. Additional information will help you learn how to develop patterns of your own design once you understand the basics.

Begin working with simple goals in mind. My first appliqués were made of corduroy and cotton velveteen. For 20 years I appliquéd corduroy with a large needle and eight stitches per inch, creating original sportswear. Those were sturdy garments able to stand repeated cleaning, even in commercial washing machines and dryers.

I later began to work with thinner fabric, smaller needles and 20 stitches per inch. I began using photographs and projectors when I wanted my appliqués to appear realistic.

Follow the methods for appliqué presented in this book and watch your own goals and skills grow.

Appliqué Tools and Supplies

The basic necessities

Fabric: 100% cotton provides easy handling for the most successful appliqués. In addition to the fabrics selected for the artistic project, plan to stock white and matching or contrasting cottons for underlining translucent fabrics.

Needles: To appliqué thin muslin-weight cottons, use a short thin needle called a *quilting/between*, size 9 or 10. To appliqué heavier fabrics such as corduroy or velveteen, use a *sharp*, size 9.

Pins: Use fine silk pins. Pins are only needed to hold the fabric in place while you baste the appliqué pieces. When you're sewing the appliqué, pins create an obstacle course, because they tangle with the thread, are in the way and add stiffness to the working area, which needs to be supple for easy manipulation.

Scissors: To cut the appliqué, use 4- or 5-inch sewing scissors, with one thin, pointed tip and one rounded blade. Use the rounded blade between the layers to prevent scissors from snagging the fabric. Cutting paper will dull fabric-scissor blades, so keep separate scissors for paper and fabric.

Thimble: Use a thimble to protect your finger tip from being pricked by the eye of the quilting needles used for appliquéing fine fabric. Explore the selection in a fabric or quilting store to find the most comfortable one; my favorite is the deerskin variety with a wide elastic band.

Thread: Baste with white or matching thread. Thread manufacturers use colorfast dyes, but dark basting thread may leave dots on a light colored fabric.

Appliqué with thread which matches the fabric piece being stitched to another fabric. It can be difficult to match thread to fabric when thread is wound on the spool. Pull a single strand across the fabric to find the closest match. The stitches will be in a shadow, so a slight shade darker is preferred to a slight shade lighter, should a perfect match be unavailable. Some guidelines for thread selection are:
    If the fabric is of animal origin, sew with silk.
    If the fabric is of plant origin, sew with cotton.

My personal preference is cotton-covered polyester thread. The strength of the polyester and the softness of the cotton make this an ideal choice. Pure cotton thread, of good quality, is a second choice. Test thread by pulling on it. If the thread can be broken without hurting your hands, it may be not be strong enough to make a durable appliqué.

Tracing paper: Onionskin typing paper works as well as tracing paper for tracing patterns from the master cartoons (drawings). For transferring the design to fabric, the softer tracing paper such as onionskin is essential. Although art-quality vellum is too brittle for my dent transfer process, it will work well for tracing photographs and for preliminary designs.

Additional useful tools

Camera: A camera can be one of the best design tools available. Take pictures of everything of interest to you. Photographs can provide information for realistic details and help to keep a diary of work in progress.

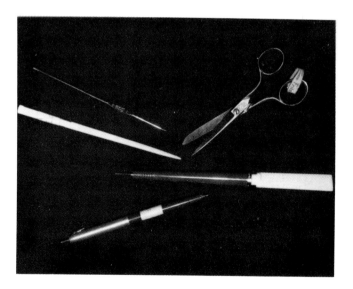

Indenting tools: I use my appliqué scissors to transfer patterns to fabric. (See "The Dent Transfer," pg. 17.) A stainless steel crochet hook, size 7, 8 or 9, is equally effective for the purpose. Stationery and office supply stores sell a *burnishing tool* which will transfer all lines to fabric except the most delicate of embroidery lines.

Magnifying tools: A magnifying lens is useful when detailing appliqués with fine embroidery. Details in photographs, such as the way eyelashes lay over an eye and the angle of skateboard struts all come to life with a magnifying lens. A printer's lupe, available at photography shops, provides eight-times magnification for close study of photos.

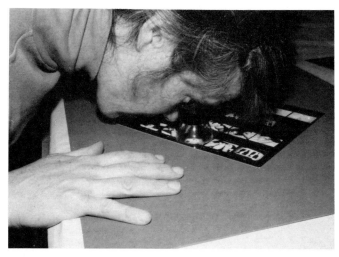

The lupe is an inexpensive magnifying lens on a short pedestal, not much larger than a spool of thread.

Newsprint: Available in very large sizes, this paper is good for large sketches, master patterns and tracings. Rolls of newsprint are available from newspaper printing plants.

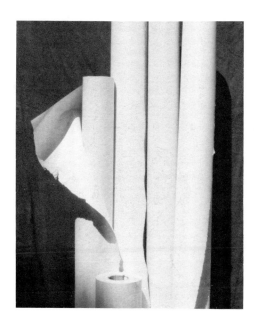

A newspaper office buys one-ton rolls which are considered scrap when they run down to fifteen pounds. Most newspaper plants give away or sell roll ends. Roll sizes most commonly available are 27 or 55 inches wide.

Photocopy machines: Use photocopy machines to enlarge or reduce images for appliqué patterns. Photocopied material is slightly distorted by some machines, due to the design of the copying mechanism, so take this into consideration when making copies which must be geometrically accurate. Plan to enlarge a complete picture before drafting pattern pieces for assembly so the pattern pieces will fit perfectly together. A standard machine will produce a maximum image of 11 x 17 inches.

Projectors: With an opaque projector, sketches and print photographs can be enlarged. Many artists refine individual elements of their drawings on separate pages, then combine them onto a master copy using an opaque projector. Opaque projectors are available in a variety of inexpensive models. Some are advertised in craft and sewing magazines. Larger opaque projectors may be purchased or can be rented from some libraries, art supply stores, and camera shops. A small projector may only enlarge a two and a half inch square photo; a large model can enlarge a six-or nine-inch photo (or sketch) into a ten- or twelve-foot picture.

A slide projector is an excellent tool for enlarging patterns. Use slides from your own photo library to generate full-sized patterns or photograph small work-sketches with slide film and then enlarge them to a desired size.

Rotary cutter and mat: A rotary blade can be used for cutting sweeping curves, straight cuts and trimming appliquéd blocks. It will cut through multiple layers more accurately than shears. A rotary cutting mat will prevent damage to your table top.

Sewing machine: Many appliqué patterns may include straight seams suitable for machine stitching.

Fabric Selection, Preparation, and Storage

Selection and preparation

Fabrics made of 100% cotton are best for hand appliqué. Cotton has a wonderful quality of being easily manipulated. Cotton can be easily creased between your fingertips to form a sharp edge for the appliqué.

A characteristic of polyester (and therefore cotton-polyester blends) is the fiber's resistance to wrinkling. For hand appliqué, this quality is a liability. Polyester is so springy that it won't stay in place when creased. It also tends to billow away from the seam when stitched.

Another benefit of cotton is that the fibers are "barbed" and a cut edge won't ravel. The cut edges of polyester (and blends) ravel and shred easily.

While cotton is the best choice for most appliqué projects, any fabric can be appliquéd. Appliqués made of velveteen and cotton corduroy are beautiful. Thinner velveteens and corduroys are easier to handle than heavier ones. The density of pile in velveteen is determined by the number of threads per inch. A fabric with thick pile is woven with fewer threads per inch. Use simpler appliqué designs with thick fabrics. Rayon velvet shreds at the edges more than cotton velveteen. It is also slippery and more difficult to handle, but beautiful and worth the challenge.

Velvet needs a larger design.

Handwoven or loosely woven fabrics can be used in appliqué. Care should be taken in choosing designs for these fabrics. Select large design elements when using large open weaves, as the loose edges of this type of fabric won't survive excessive handling. Sew handwoven fabrics with a large needle, ¼" hem allowances and fewer stitches per inch. Wool fabrics such as melton or flannel are easy to use. Wool handles much like finer cotton weaves.

To use my dent transfer technique, use 100% cotton fabric – finely woven, soft-finished, solid colors. As you become accustomed to reading the dent transfer markings on the fabric, you can begin using printed fabrics. Always select fabrics of high quality.

Preshrink every fabric as soon as you bring it home. Cottons can shrink as much as 10% when washed and dried.

Colorfastness is an important consideration when planning appliqué. To test the color fastness of fabrics, place each piece separately in a bath of very warm water. After five minutes, dip a white cup into the water for a sample and observe whether the dye has tinted the water.

I like to keep an accurate inventory of my fabrics. I include notations as to which fabrics bled dye during testing and which did not; the bleeding fabrics go into projects which will never be washed. You may wish to keep a similar inventory.

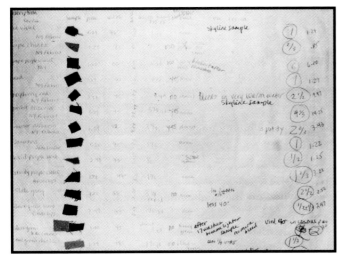

This inventory includes the purchase price and the yardage.

Storage:

To avoid fold lines in fabrics, I drape my large pieces of fabric over wooden poles, full width across and several layers deep. These poles fit into a slotted wood rack mounted on a wall. This keeps the fabric conveniently available for use. The hanging layers can be turned like pages in a book.

In limited space, hang fabrics many layers deep on a few poles.

To protect the fabrics from fading in sunlight or fluorescent light, place a sheet of clean muslin over them.

Hanging storage does more than prevent creases in fabrics. It also allows air circulation and prevents mildew.

Small fabric scraps are easier to store and find in file folders. Divide scraps into color families with a folder for each – blue in one, yellow in another, red in still another. Sorting through scraps then becomes a neat and easy task.

The folders keep fabrics clean and flat.

Glossary of Special Terms

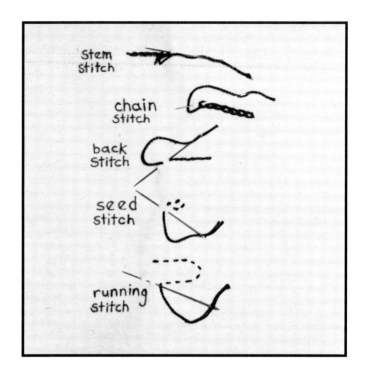

Anchor stitches – stitches that begin and end a line of appliqué. Each thread, unknotted, is anchored in fabric with three small backstitches taken next to each other.

Basting – taking large stitches to temporarily join two or more pieces of fabric. Begin and end a basting row with at least two backstitches. Baste with running stitches, which may be ¼" long for joining small fabric pieces, or two inches long for joining large fabric pieces.

Cartoon – a full-size drawing of all the outlines and detail lines to be appliquéd and embroidered in a project. The cartoon is the master pattern which remains intact, to be used as a roadmap to guide the assembly of the appliqué. Fabric grain lines are marked on the various portions of the design, parallel to the side edges of the cartoon. All pattern pieces are traced individually from this cartoon.

Dagger points – the outside corners which are so narrow that it seems unlikely two hem allowances will fit under the appliquéd points.

Dent transfer – the method used to transfer appliqué patterns onto the fabric by indenting the surface of fabric. The indentations are made by drawing with a bluntly pointed tool, such as a stainless steel crochet hook (size six through nine), over a soft, onionskin paper pattern held on top of the fabric.

Detail stitches – delicate embroidery stitches used to "draw" fine detail lines on appliqué.

Grain line – direction of thread woven into fabric. The woven thread lines parallel to the selvage are those "straight of the grain." Those threads running at right angles to the selvage are "cross grain." A 45° diagonal to the selvage is "bias" to the grain, and very stretchy. Generally the straight grain of the fabric should run parallel to the side edges of the appliqué for optimal strength and minimal stretch. Draw a grain line on each piece of the paper pattern to align with the straight grain of the fabric when transferring the pattern.

Hem allowance – the narrow portion of fabric, between the stitching line and the cut edge, to be turned under.

Inside corner – a corner cut into the body of fabric.

Inside curve – a shape often referred to as a concave curve. This shape cuts into the body of fabric and needs to be clipped at the hem edge before the hem allowance will fold under.

Lupe – a magnifying glass on a pedestal, about the size of a spool of thread. The lupe is placed on a photograph or drawing, to be looked through with the eye positioned against the magnifier.

Matching-arrows – small marks in a hem allowance or seam allowance used to correctly position two fabric edges for stitching. Use the pin matching technique to align these marks.

Matching-line – the portion of the appliqué stitching line which has another appliqué piece stitched exactly onto it. The matching-line has an extra large allowance drawn outside it; this allowance is called the under-layer flap.

Outside corner – a corner jutting out from the body of fabric.

Outside curve – also known as a convex curve. This curve has an outward shape like a circle or sphere, and is left unclipped for hemming.

Pin-matching – a method used to position pieces. Insert two pins so they pierce the stitching line at points A and B; then pierce through corresponding points A and B of a matching-line on a second piece of fabric. Slide the two fabrics together along the pins. The two stitching lines and the points A and points B will be positioned precisely upon each other, ready for basting.

Reverse appliqué – with layers of fabric basted upon each other, a design is cut through successive layers to reveal the various fabrics. Each layer is appliquéd to the next layer in the sandwich.

Rolling a curve – turning hem allowances inside a hairpin curve (and inside a corner) using more than gentle tucking with a needle tip. To achieve a smooth hem edge free of ravels, roll the hem under with the *shaft* of the stitching needle. Rolling the hem *forcefully* puts more fabric into the hem allowance, bending the hem edge well past the clips taken in the allowance. Tenderly tucking the allowance of extreme curves and inside corners results in the hem's barely being folded under at the clips, allowing the edge to appear raveled.

Stitch length – number of stitches per inch. There is a minimum formula for appliqué stitch length, based on depth of the hem allowance. For example, if using a $\frac{1}{4}$" hem, take four stitches per inch; if using fewer than four stitches, the hem will pull out from between the stitches. An $\frac{1}{8}$" allowance requires at least eight stitches per inch; a $\frac{1}{16}$" allowance uses at least sixteen stitches per inch, and so forth.

Aesthetic standards are more demanding. Stitching should be invisible. If $\frac{1}{8}$" is turned under, fourteen to twenty stitches per inch will be less visible. When the folded edge will be $\frac{1}{16}$" wide use up to thirty stitches per inch.

Trace – Trace the pattern pieces on onionskin paper from the original cartoon, using a pencil. Outlines and important details can be traced on transparent paper from photographs when planning the cartoon.

Transfer – draw the pattern on fabric with the dent transfer technique.

Under-layer flap – an extra fabric allowance, a flap as large as a thumbprint to which an upper layer of appliqué fabric can be basted. This under-layer flap may be designed to remain underneath the appliqué as padding for extra dimension. The under-layer flap may be trimmed to $\frac{1}{8}$" after appliqué stitching is completed on that piece of fabric, to reduce bulk.

Underlining – a second fabric cut to the shape of an appliqué piece, without added hem allowances. This lining is used under white and pastel fabrics to prevent other back layers of fabric and thread from shadowing through. Underlinings are basted to the corresponding appliqué fabric and both fabrics are then stitched as one piece. Embroidered details for the appliqué are stitched through both these layers of fabric at the same time. A colored underlining may also be used, to intentionally shadow the top fabric. A white or matching colored underlining will block shadowing.

Walk a pin – move a single pin securing the turned edge of fabric an inch ahead of the stitches last made. Stitch toward the pin, remove pin before it is reached, fine-tune the tucked edge with the needle, re-pin and stitch toward pin. Walk the pin ahead of the stitching this way to hold the far end of a curve or to hold long, straight edges.

Basic Appliqué Techniques

Supplies needed

Two solid-colored pieces of fabric
        4" x 6" for appliqué
        6" x 8" for background
Sewing needle: quilting, size 10
Thread to match appliqué fabric
Small, sharp scissors
Thimble
Two or three fine pins

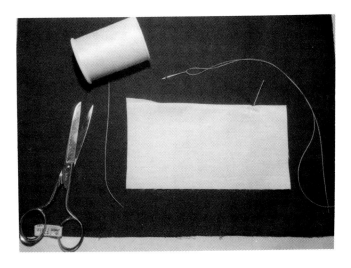

To begin

1. Hold the edge of the appliqué fabric piece. Fold ⅛" of the top edge to the back.

2. Pin the folded edge of fabric to the middle of the background fabric. The folded edge should be at the top of the layout.

3. Thread a needle. Leave the thread unknotted.

4. Run a finger tip or the back of an index fingernail along edge of fold. This will crease the fabric fold. This crease will remain long enough for it to be sewn down. This step is called *finger pressing.*

The following directions are from a right-handed perspective. Stitching direction will be from the right-hand edge of fabric to the left. Left-handed stitchers should work from left to right.

Anchor stitches

5. Lift the upper right-hand edge of the folded fabric. Turn this fabric back ¼" to reveal the background fabric behind the appliqué. Insert the needle into the background fabric behind the appliqué fabric so the anchor stitches will be hidden by the appliqué. With the tip of the needle lift two threads of background fabric. Pull the needle and thread through, leaving a ¼" thread tail.

6. Take three ¹⁄₁₆" long backstitches. These stitches should be side-by-side. Form these stitches where they will not show. Each backstitch begins where the previous stitch began, near but not exactly in, the same hole. The stitches may appear parallel to each other or they may resemble a bird footprint; either way is correct.

Draw the thread through these three stitches completely each time. Pull on the thread after the third stitch to make sure the thread is secure. Using only two stitches will allow the thread to pull loose. Three tiny anchor stitches begin and end every appliqué seam.

Holding the work

When stitching right handed, hold the fabric in the left hand. To hold small appliqué pieces, place the left thumb and forefinger above the work and the other three fingers below. Hold the fabric where it will be stitched.

The left thumbnail helps by holding the folded edge just below the fold. Press the thumb against the middle finger with the thumbnail $1/20$ of an inch from the folded edge, leaving the index finger free to manipulate the fabric edge from above.

When holding larger pieces, it may not be possible to fit all the fabric between these two fingers. Then the index finger must be below the fabric. In that case, the index finger is opposite the thumb. The ring finger can hold the fabric with the little finger, providing a bit of tension to make stitching easier.

These maneuvers may seem awkward when reading them, but if put into practice they soon become automatic.

7. Place the folded edge back onto the background fabric.

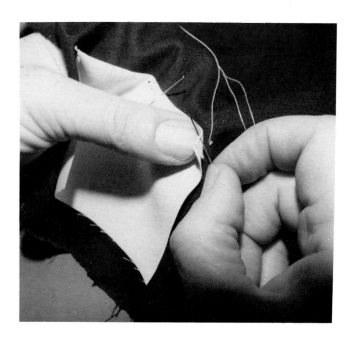

The appliqué stitch

8. Slip the needle through the folded edge from the hem to the front layer of the appliqué fabric.

The needle tip should be two threads from the folded edge.

9. Begin to stitch. Insert your needle tip into the background fabric nearest the place where the thread emerges and perpendicular to the folded edge.

Do not travel even a slight diagonal forward before this stitch.

With your needle tip behind all layers, direct the tip diagonally ahead of the stitching line, traveling about $1/16$" to $1/8$".

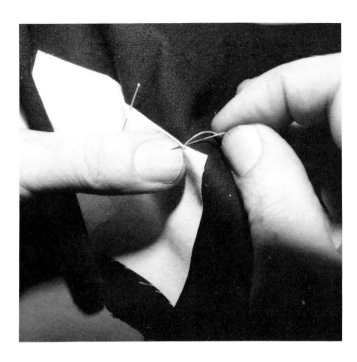

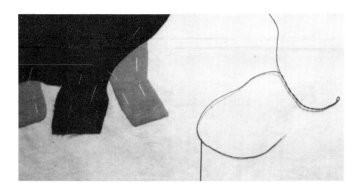

Bring the needle to the front of work through all layers, two threads from the fold. Repeat this stitch, working from right to left. A row of diagonal stitches will show on the back of the work.

When looking at the front of the work, you will see only very small perpendicular stitches.

Thread develops a twist as you stitch. When it becomes apparent, twist the needle in the opposite direction as you stitch, or drop the needle and let the thread spin itself back to its relaxed condition.

End the row of stitching as you began, with three short anchor stitches in place. This time the stitches should be taken on the back of the work.

Start with easy shapes and practice stitching techniques; then progress to more intricate shapes. Throughout this book and in the section at the back are projects and patterns to be used to build skill and confidence. Both start simply and become progressively more complicated.

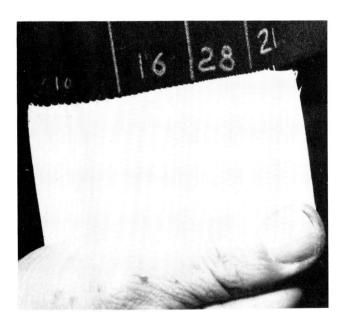

Stitches secure the appliqué. Are your stitches close enough?

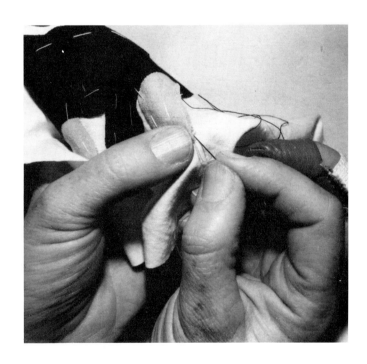

The Dent Transfer

Transfer of patterns to fabric is done by the dent transfer. One advantage of the dent transfer technique is that these markings leave no permanent evidence, unlike pen lines which may never come out of the fabric or pencil lines which require thorough washing for removal. Another advantage is that the exact stitching line is transferred, allowing for extreme accuracy.

To practice using the dent transfer, choose a solid colored scrap of soft cotton fabric. Lay one layer of the fabric, right side up, on a hard, smooth table top or surface, such as glass, masonite or a cutting mat. Use a pencil to draw a slightly wavy line on the onionskin paper. Place the paper over the fabric scrap.

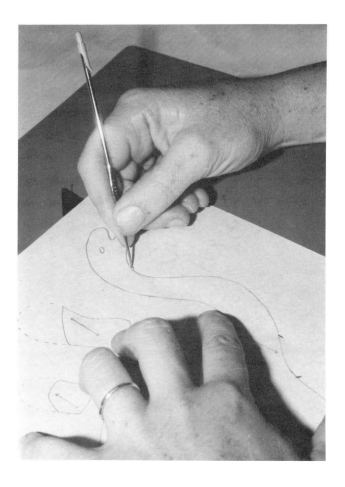

Hold the scissors as if they were a pencil. To transfer a marking to the fabric, press very firmly with the *rounded* tip of the closed scissors and trace over the line drawn on the paper so that an indentation goes through to the fabric. The *sharp* tip of the scissors will shred the paper and damage the fabric.

Use a small stainless steel crochet hook (size 7, 8 or 9) if rounded tip scissors are not available.

Experiment with a graphic artist's burnishing tool and other bluntly pointed instruments. Take care not to rip through the paper with these tools.

Remove the paper and look for the indentation on the fabric surface.

The "dent" will show on solid-colored cotton if you pressed firmly enough. With practice, the dent will be visible on printed fabric, polished cottons (or, if necessary, polyester blends). The dent shows well on corduroy and cotton velveteen.

If a print fabric is too busy to reveal the dent, then indent the pattern on muslin, flatten the muslin on top of the print fabric, and cut both fabrics as if they were one.

The dent will remain in the fabric, even if pressed with a steam iron, until it is removed by *dampening* the line.

Experimenting with Color

Fabric play

Assemble a selection of different solid colored fabrics, each piece about twelve inches square. Lay these fabrics next to and overlapping each other. Stand back from the color arrangement. Look at the combinations and ask these questions for each combination:

Do the fabrics contrast?
Do the colors have a pleasant relationship?
Do the colors fight for attention?
Which colors jump out?
Which colors recede?

Try more color combinations answering the above questions. Observe how different combinations make the color values change dramatically. Some colors won't work as background because they overpower colors placed on them. Some colors are strong, but work well *in combination* with others, even as background. Some colors work in combination in one area, but add confusion when used in other areas. The use of color and value is subjective. With a little experimentation you will see what is best for you.

Basic color relationships

Colors which come forward are called hot colors. Colors that recede are called cool colors. One color can be cool or hot depending on the colors juxtaposed in the relationship. Red is a hot color. Some reds are hotter than others. Red can be a blue-red (cool) or an orange-red (hot). If a project calls for red in several areas, use the coolest one in the background. Generally speaking, blue is a cool color. Observe how colors change in relation to other colors in the appliqué. Fabric colors are affected by the others they are placed next to.

The easiest way to plan color schemes is to lay colors together on a table. Stand back, observe and make changes. No amount of theory will substitute for practice. Unity can be achieved by repeating colors or changing the tints and shades. Black, white, or gray can be used for contrast. Black makes pale colors brilliant. White turns dark colors to jewel tones. Gray will quiet colors.

The placement of repeated colors is important. Three points of the same color separated by a wide triangular space will unite the design. If one color is used as an accent, integrate it in some way elsewhere in the design.

Just as colors can appear hot or cold, they can also appear to have weight. Dark colors are heavy. Pastel colors are light. Be aware of the weight of colors as they are being combined. If a flat effect is desired, distribute heavy colors throughout the design. To achieve perspective, make sure the heavy colors are "on the ground."

Take your time in selecting colors, as the combinations selected can make a great difference in the overall success of a design.

Appliquéing a Sampler Shape

This is a quick project to introduce handling techniques for common design shapes. All the shapes included in this side view of a "head" with a vertical "antler" are found in the appliqué projects elsewhere in this book, so it will be helpful to practice them here. Other shapes to be encountered in any appliqué project will be some combination of the shapes in this sampler.

Supplies needed

Two 4"x 5" pieces of 100% cotton fabric, contrasting solid colors
Thread to match color selected for appliqué shape
Quilting needles: size 9 or 10, also size 12
Stainless steel crochet hook, size 7, 8 or 9, or indenting tool of choice
Small, sharp scissors
Onionskin paper, 4" x 5"
Pencil
Thimble
One pin

To begin

1. Trace the basic appliqué sampler shape pattern from the pattern section of book (pg. 56), on onionskin paper.

2. Place the single layer of fabric to be cut into the shape on a smooth, hard work surface. Position the onionskin tracing over the fabric. Match the straight horizontal line on the bottom of the shape to a straight thread of the fabric (cross grain or straight grain). Using the dent transfer technique, transfer the stitching lines of the pattern to the fabric with the tool. Press very firmly through the paper. Transfer the eye shape as well as the outline. Do not transfer clipping or cutting lines; use them for a visual guide.

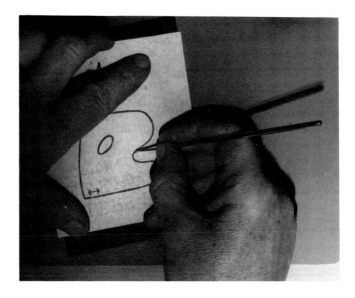

Hold the crochet hook like a pencil to use the dent transfer technique for marking pattern on fabric.

3. Cut the sampler shape ⅛" outside the stitching line indentation. Train your eye to estimate the ⅛" hem allowance. Insert scissor tip into the fabric in the center of the eye and snip through a thread or two.

Clip inside curves and inside corner

Here is a guide for clipping the sampler shape:

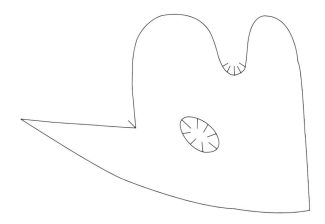

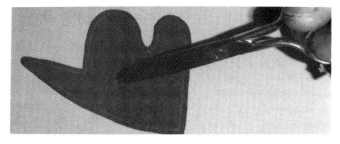

1. Clip the eye from the snipped hole, stopping two threads short of the marked stitching line. Make eight small clips, one at each narrow end and three along each longer edge. Every clip radiates from the center snip and aims perpendicular to the stitching line.

2. Clip the inward corner where top of head becomes bottom of antler. Clip from the exact cut corner to the exact stitching line corner, stopping the clip one thread from the stitching line.

3. Clip the inside hairpin curve of the mouth, starting where the line actually curves, rather than at the beginning of the mouth. The clips are ⅛" apart, perpendicular to the stitching line, stopping two threads from the marked stitching line. The middle three clips may radiate from a single location of the cut edge. Once the curve starts to straighten, stop clipping.

4. Outside curves are not to be clipped.

5. Trim the hem allowance on the sides of the dagger point at the tip of the antler to 1/12" wide. Round the very tip, leaving it ⅛" longer than the marked point.

Baste the shape to the background

1. Position the appliqué shape on the background fabric, centering it and matching the grain lines of both fabrics to each other. The left-handed stitcher should reverse the shape so the appliqué directions can be followed in the order presented.

2. Thread the size 9 or 10 quilting needle with a 15" length of white thread or thread matching the appliqué fabric. Begin ⅜" from the cut edges at the square corner. Take two ¼" backstitches by taking one stitch, then another in the same place. Backstitches eliminate the need for a knot at the end of thread.

3. Take ½" long running stitches to baste the shape ⅜" from the cut edge, up the long side, toward the antler. The antler is narrower than the rest of the sampler shape, so place the basting stitches through its middle and back down the same middle. Baste ⅜" from the nose, around the outside curve. The hairpin curve inside the mouth should be basted farther from the cut edges to leave room for the needle to manipulate the hem allowance, so baste ½" from the hairpin curve. Continue basting across the bottom of the shape, ending with two backstitches. Cut basting thread leaving ¼" tail of thread at the fabric.

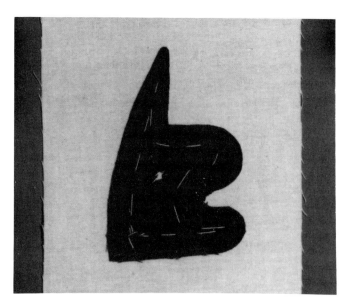

The basic appliqué sampler shape basted to the background fabric.

Anchor the thread in the stitching line

Re-thread needle with a 15" length of thread matching the appliqué fabric. Leave the thread unknotted. Begin the appliqué stitching at the bottom square corner. Hold the basted pieces in the non-sewing hand, with the stitching edge "at the top of the page." Finger press this straight edge along the marked stitching line, folding the hem allowance under the appliqué fabric.

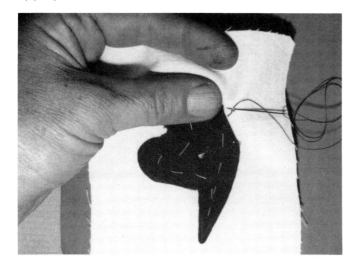

Lift the edge and take three anchor stitches. The anchor stitches will be hidden beneath the appliqué when the shape is finished. Tug the thread gently to be sure it is secure.

Appliqué the shape to the background

Return the edge of appliqué fabric to the surface of the background. Use your needle tip to help fold the hem allowance under the fabric, repeating this needle tucking after every few stitches throughout the appliqué.

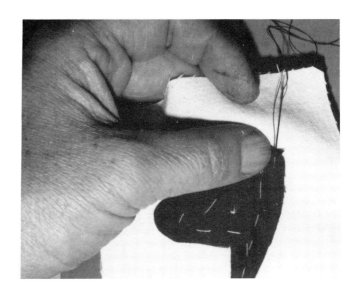

Bring the needle to the front of the work, through the folded edge at the marked corner of the stitching lines.

Begin stitching where the indentations for the bottom edge and long side meet, leaving the long side hem allowance free of stitches. Appliqué according to instructions in the chapter "Basic Appliqué Techniques" (pg. 14).

Pull all stitches snugly to sink the thread into the weave of the fabric.

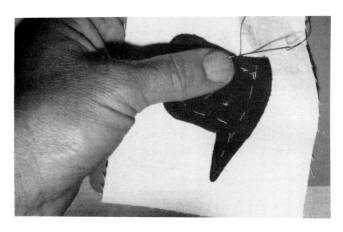

The correct appliqué stitch is taken in one step, in and out of the fabrics without stopping between the background and the appliqué fabric.

Continue stitching, watching that each stitch is a short perpendicular over the front edge of the fold, and a slightly longer diagonal across the wrong side of the background fabric.

Stitch around the curves of the mouth

Ease the extra hem allowance under the outside curve of the chin, and later the nose, to smooth it under the appliqué. As each ¼" section of the appliqué hem allowance is tucked under the appliqué, graze the fabric of the allowance with the needle tip and gently slide the allowance back toward the last stitches taken. Stitch that ¼" section.

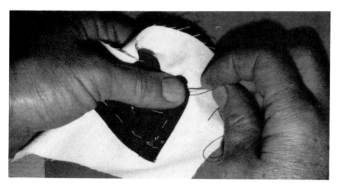

Tuck, ease, and stitch again until the outside curve is completed.

Stitch inside the hairpin curve

Standard hem allowances for appliqué are ⅛" to ¹⁄₁₂". Inside the hairpin curve of the mouth, the allowance is turned ¹⁄₂₀" *beyond the clips.* The stitches will be 20 to 30 per inch, close enough to secure the edge of a smoothly curved shape.

1. Refrain from stitching once the chin begins to enter the mouth. Pin the nose to the background, matching the fabric grain lines of the nose and background. The pin adds extra stability to the upper end of this curve as it is shaped before stitching.

2. Prepare the inside curve before stitching into it. Use the *shaft* of the needle to firmly roll the hem allowance under the hairpin curve, far enough beyond the clips to achieve a perfectly smooth and rounded edge.

If enough pressure is used in rolling the inside hairpin curve, a perfect curve will be easy to achieve.

Roll from the upper edge of the mouth toward the chin and then roll back again. Repeat as needed until the perfect round is found. The only way this inside curve will have a frayed edge is if the hem is not rolled far enough under the appliqué. If the edge doesn't turn under enough as it is rolled, then the motion used is too delicate; roll again more firmly. If the curve rolls far enough but has a flat "facet" anywhere, then the hem allowance at the facet needs to be clipped closer to the stitching line. Only one more thread may need to be clipped, so proceed carefully.

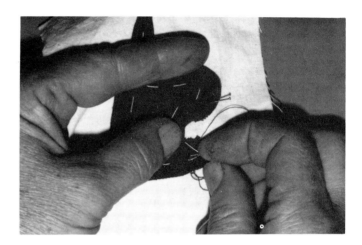

3. When the inside curve is defined, press the edge once under a finger tip. This pressing is a guideline, but the hem will need to be fine-tuned with the needle as the mouth curve is stitched.

4. At the chin, use the needle tip between the appliqué front and its hem allowance to ease some of the fabric to the front edge if necessary. In the hairpin-turning some extra fabric may have gotten tucked into the allowance. The lower edge of the mouth should have ¹⁄₁₂" to ⅛" hem allowance, with a graceful stitching line heading into the mouth.

5. Appliqué the inside of the mouth with close stitches, correcting the folded hem as needed. Remove the pin from the nose.

Appliqué the inside corner

1. Appliqué the outside curve of the nose, easing the allowance with the needle tip grazing the hem between the layers. Stitch to within ¼" of the inside corner between the top of the head and the antler.

2. Use the needle *shaft* to tuck under the hem allowance on the antler side of the corner. Roll the hem firmly past the clip at the corner, forcing under at least two threads past the cut.

3. Rolling the corner under will also roll the last ¼" of hem not yet stitched along the head before the corner. Use the needle tip to lift the folded edge back into a straight line to the corner from the last stitch taken. Stitch to the corner, tucking the edge again with the shaft if necessary; take one stitch precisely in the corner.

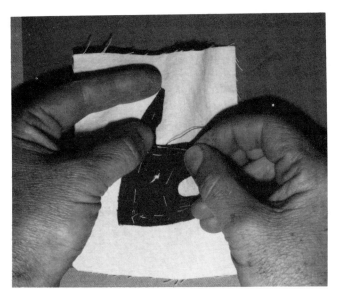

Force under at least two threads past the clipped inside corner. Use your needle tip to lift the folded edge of the hem back to the stitching line and shape the square corner.

Appliqué the "dagger point"

The outside corner of the antler is a "dagger point." The hem allowance at this point should be trimmed to ¹⁄₁₂". The very tip of the hem allowance should be trimmed so that ⅛" of the hem extends beyond the stitching line point. Round the allowance at the tip.

1. To prevent fraying of the tip, stitch with the thinnest needle possible, ideally a quilting needle, size 12.

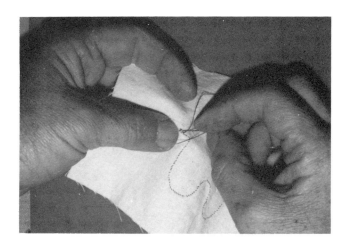

On the wrong side of the block, anchor your thread behind the work, near the stitching line. Re-thread a fresh 15" length of thread to finish the appliqué. Anchor the new thread next to end of the previous thread, behind the appliqué background.

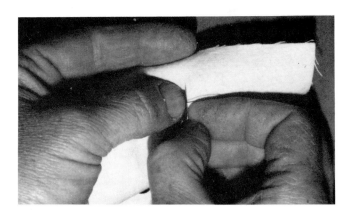

Tuck the hem allowance under with the needle shaft. Stitch up one side of the point, taking a stitch exactly at the point where indented stitching lines converge.

2. With the needle *shaft*, tuck under the allowance on the other side of the point, from about ¾" from tip, working toward the tip.

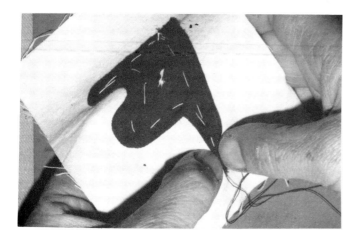

Finger crease between the back of your thumbnails, along the stitching indentation, to the intended tip, regardless of whether or not the hem allowance easily fits under the appliqué at this stage.

3. Use the needle shaft rather than the needle tip to bend the hem allowance at the tip of the dagger point around and under the appliqué point. Assist the needle with your index finger tip.

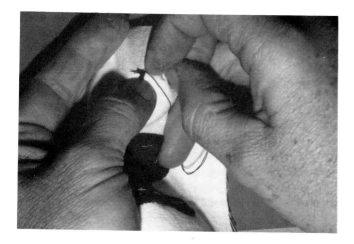

Pivot the allowance smoothly so the shape's edge can continue in the opposite direction, with no curling nor cramming of the tip.

4. The extra layers of fabric will be encapsulated by the stitches taken at the point, so it is not helpful to fuss at the hem allowance with the needle tip. Narrow points are the exceptional circumstance where the appliqué stitch *is* taken in two steps. First take the half of the stitch in which the needle lifts two threads from the background fabric. Pull the needle and thread through this half-stitch.

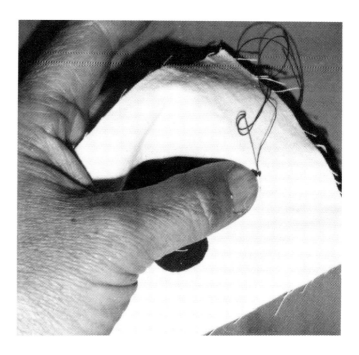

Make the second half of the appliqué stitch, inserting the needle into the folded edge of top layer fabric, $\frac{1}{12}$" from the tip's edge. Catch none of the extra hem allowances that are congregating under the fabric point. Pull this stitch snug. Take two more stitches around tip in this same manner.

5. Inspect the appliqué point. To be most secure, it probably needs another stitch inserted between each of the last three or four stitches taken, one of these in the exact tip of the point and some on both sides of the point.

6. Finish stitching the second side of the point in the normal, one-step appliqué stitch. Before continuing far beyond the point, set the needle down and return your attention to the point.

Using the backs of the thumbnails, squeeze the tip to crease the point once more. The fabric in the point will reshape vertically, where before it lay closer to the background fabric. Continue the appliqué, changing back to the size 9 or 10 needle.

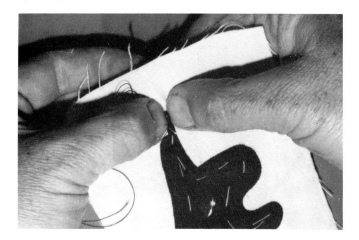

Complete the square corner

The square corner is the last shape to complete the outline of the sampler. The hem allowance at the bottom edge of the shape has already been turned to begin the sampler.

1. Turn the corner of the already folded edge under the square of the appliqué. Slip the tip of the needle between the applique hem and the background.

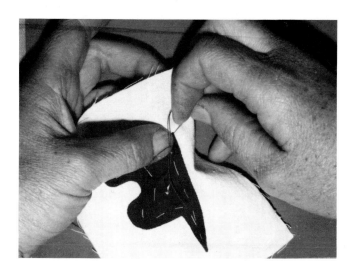

Prick the folded hem corner and slide it snugly against the side of the corner that has already been stitched. Smooth the hem between the layers if it has bunched.

2. Stitch to the corner. Take a last stitch exactly into the corner, and remain on the back side of the background fabric. Anchor the thread with the three backstitches like those which began the appliqué. Cut the thread and remove the basting stitches.

Stitch the eye in reverse appliqué

1. Thread the size 10 needle with 10" of fresh, unknotted thread. Anchor it behind the appliqué, next to the stitching line nearest the eye. Make certain the anchor stitches are placed where they will not show on the front of the appliqué.

2. Insert the needle through the background at the anchor stitches, between the layers, and out through the clipped eye hole. The needle should not enter the appliqué fabric yet.

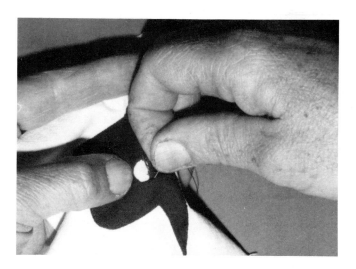

With the shaft of the needle, roll the entire eye hem allowance under, using the same firm touch that was needed when the inside mouth was turned. When the eye hem allowance has been turned 1/20" beyond the clipped edge, press with a finger tip.

3. Slip the needle through folded edge to the front of the appliqué, two threads from the finger-pressed edge. Appliqué the eye, re-tucking the eye hem allowance as needed to maintain the smooth curves.

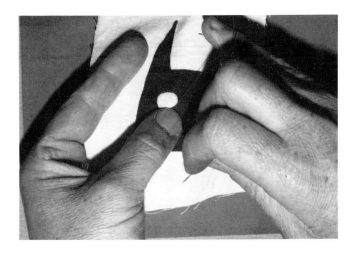

The little finger of the needle hand applies tension on the thread to pull an eye stitch snugly against the folded hem.

4. After the last stitch, slip the needle between the fabric layers again, to return to the back of the appliqué near the eye stitches. Anchor the thread. Cut the thread.

Fuchsia Appliqué Project

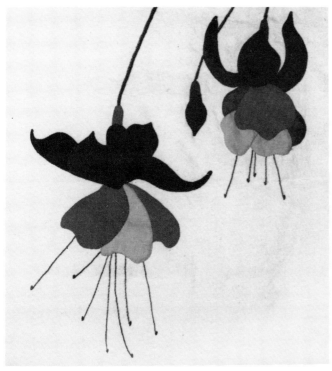

Instructions for completing the blossom and bud on the right are provided in this chapter. The second blossom can be made in conjunction with the following chapter.

Supplies needed

Quilting needles: size 10 and size 12
Small, sharp scissors
Two sheets of onionskin paper
Pencil
Indenting tool such as a stainless steel crochet hook:
    size 7, 8 or 9
Three fine pins
100% cotton fabric in solid colors as follows:
    five pieces 6" x 6", one each in three shades of
        pink, one bright red and one dark red
    one piece 2" x 2", green
    one piece 12" x 12" for the background, in a
        contrasting color
Thread to match each appliqué fabric
White thread for basting
30" of six-strand embroidery thread in each of two
    shades of green
15" of six-strand embroidery thread in each of three
    shades of dark pink and/or red

Transfer pattern to fabrics

1. Trace pattern pieces (page 58) on the onionskin paper.

2. Place the light pink fabric directly on a hard, smooth, work surface. Lay the page of onionskin over the fabric, matching the grain line arrow on pattern piece #2 with the straight grain of the fabric. Leave room on the fabric for the ⅛" hem allowance which will be cut around the petal design and for a petal to be cut from pattern piece #3.

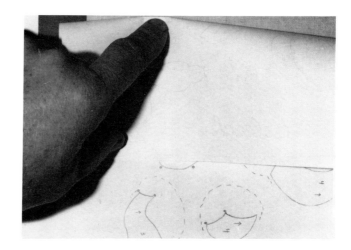

Crease a ¼" long fold along the drawn grain line on the paper. Lift the edge of the paper to match the crease to the fabric thread grain. You can hold the flat edge of your burnishing tool on the marked grain line and then lift the paper to observe placement on the appliqué fabric.

The flat edge of a burnishing tool is held to the paper, on the marked grain line, and the paper is lifted to observe placement on the appliqué fabric.

3. Hold the pattern paper carefully and firmly on the fabric. Hold the indenting tool as you would a pencil. Apply very firm pressure to draw the solid line defining the finished appliqué shape. This line is the exact stitching line.

Still holding the paper to the fabric, transfer the under-layer flap outline as a solid line (even though it appears on the pattern as a dotted line), and transfer the matching-arrows to just outside of the stitching line. Where the under-layer flap is drawn surrounding a part of the stitching line, that stitching line becomes the matching-line for the adjoining appliqué.

Do not transfer grain line arrows to the fabric. Also, the clipping lines in the hem allowances of the pattern are only for visual reference, and are not to be transferred.

4. Transfer all remaining pattern pieces to fabric, using the middle shade of pink for piece #5, the dark shade of pink for pieces #1 and #4, bright red for pieces #6, #9 and #11, dark red for pieces #7 and #8, green for pieces #10 and #12. Matching-arrows should be transferred to the hem allowance as simple straight lines, perpendicular to the stitching line.

Cut appliqué pieces and clip the hem allowances

1. Carefully cut all pieces of fabric, adding a ⅛" hem allowance outside all stitching lines.

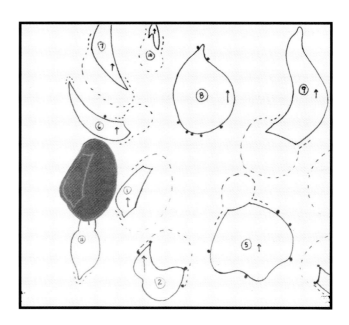

Under-layer flaps need the added hem allowance only for the first ⅛" beyond the matching-lines, since the whole flap is an exaggerated allowance already.

2. Clip the inside curves with small snips of the scissors halfway into the hem allowance, ⅛" to ¼" apart. Clips described as shallow clips should only cut ¼ of the hem depth. Stop clipping when the curves begin to straighten out or become outside curves. Refer to the pattern in the pattern section of this book to plan the location of clips.

piece #1 needs one clip,
piece #2 needs one clip,
piece #3 needs two shallow clips,
piece #4 needs no clips,
piece #5 needs three clips in the deeper curve and two very shallow clips on the shallow curve,
piece #6 needs five shallow clips,
piece #7 needs five shallow clips,
piece #8 needs three clips on the longer curve and one clip on the little curve at its tip,
piece #9 needs three shallow clips on the right-hand curve, two shallow clips on the short left-hand

curve, and seven clips on the long curve,
piece #11, the bud, needs a clip at each inside corner before the swelling and two shallow clips at each side of the tip.
The green pieces (#10 and #12) need no clips.

Review colors selected

Refer to the cartoon of the fuchsia on page 59; position all pieces of fabric on each other as they will appear when complete. The uppermost layer will be piece #8, next will be pieces #5 and #6, next will be #7, #9 and #2, then #3, and finally #1 and #4. The bud beside the fuchsia flower will have the red piece #11 on top of green #12. If a fabric color selection appears out of place now that all pieces are positioned, this is the time to find another shade and re-cut the appliqué piece.

Seeing the pieces in place will make assembly of the fuchsia unit much easier.

Clues for stitching curves

Review the chapter "Appliquéing a Sampler Shape" (page 19) for illustrations of these guidelines.

As carefully as a design outline may be planned, it is the depth and frequency of clips which finally determine the shape of the inside curves. Suggestions for

clipping the inside curves are on the previous page. When tucking the curved hem allowances, be sure that all clips are fully hidden by the folded edge, even if that requires altering a planned stitching line.

All inside curves, especially severe, hairpin-type curves, will be improved by rolling the hem under the entire curve before beginning to stitch any of it. Sometimes the curve planned is not the curve as the clips define it; therefore the angle of the folded hem approaching the curve will take a slightly different direction than planned. The shaft of the needle is rolled against the foldline of hem to shape inside curves.

Outside curves will be stitched with ⅛" hem allowances or narrower and will need no clipping since the allowance is small enough to add little bulk. However, because there is more fabric surface being tucked under the appliqué than there is before the fold, it is possible to accidentally fold little pleats into the hem allowance. To avoid the pleats, every time the next quarter-inch of hem is folded under, gently grab the hem with the needle tip and slide it back toward the last stitch, easing the extra fabric under the appliqué.

Assemble the fuchsia unit

Hold the appliqué with the stitching line "at the top of the page" while stitching. If necessary refer to the chapters "Basic Appliqué Techniques" and "Basic Shapes Appliqué Sampler," where all the stitching techniques are illustrated.

1. Select the appliqué pieces #2 and #1. Place petal #2 over petal #1, right sides up. Use this pin-matching technique to match the stitching lines AB: pierce stitching line AB of petal #2 with a pin at the matching-arrow A and a pin at matching-arrow B.

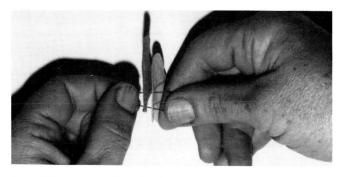

Insert the same pins into the corresponding matching-arrows on petal #1.

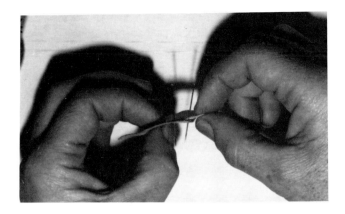

Slide the petals together along the pins until they touch, matching the marked stitching lines exactly.

With a third pin, join the two pieces of fabric through the overlapping portions: petal #2 and under-layer flap #1. Remove matching pins. Using white thread in the size 10 needle, baste the petals together through the under-layer flap with ¼" long stitches. Begin and end the basting row with two backstitches. Cut thread and remove pin.

2. Re-thread needle with an 8" length of light pink thread to match petal #2.

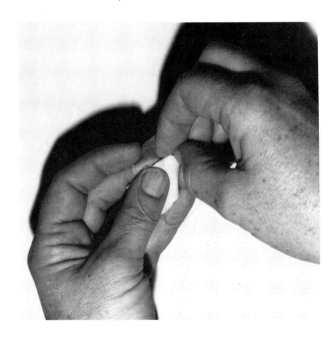

In the flap of #1 near A, take three small anchor stitches, within ⅛" of stitching line AB. Appliqué petal #2 to #1. The last stitch of this line should be taken exactly at B, where another stitching line of petal #1 meets the matching line.

The hem allowance of petal #1 must remain free of stitches so that it will be loose to turn under when stitching the appliqué to the background later.
The stitch taken in the corner B will be only half a stitch, as the needle will remain behind the under-layer, not re-emerging to the front of the work. Take three anchor stitches behind the work, at point B, next to the stitching line within the first ⅛" of the under-layer flap. Cut the thread, trim the under-layer flap to ⅛". Remove the basting stitches.

3. Join petal #2 over petal #3 using the same method.

Join petal #3 to #4, matching thread to petal #3.

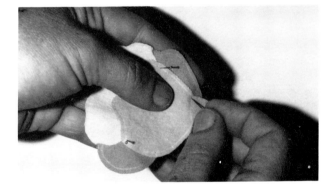

Place Petal #5 over assembly of petals #1-4. Pin-match stitching lines GA and arrows E.

4. Under-layer flaps may be trimmed to ¼" (next to stitching lines already taken only) if they inhibit smooth assembly of the next piece. Appliqué petal #5 to the assembly of petals #1-4. The matching-arrows of petal #5 should align with the stitching lines just completed in the first four petals.

Notice the under-layer flap being held out of the way by free fingers of the holding hand, and thread being tensioned with the little finger of needle hand to "snug" the stitch into fabric.

Trim under-layers when petal #5 is secure. Leave stitches unsnipped.

5. Appliqué red piece #6 on red piece #7, matching the point and arrow labeled H. Trim flap to ⅛". Appliqué #5 to piece #9.

6. Appliqué piece #8 over #6-7. Without cutting the red thread from the appliqué, re-thread needle and baste #8 to #1-5-9. Re-thread needle with the red appliqué thread. Resume stitching #8, this time to #1-5-9, turning hem allowance of #6 at J as this step is begun.

Baste the fuchsia petal #8 to the green piece #10. Baste bud piece #11 over green piece #12.

Appliqué the fuchsia assembly to the background

1. Trace to the second sheet of onionskin paper the outermost outline of the fuchsia and the bud, found on the master cartoon in the pattern section. Trace the embroidery lines for the stems and stamen. Trace the right-hand edge of the cartoon page to use as a grain line matching-line when placing the paper on the background fabric.

2. Place the onionskin paper over the background fabric, positioning the fuchsia pattern in the upper right-hand section of background. Match the grain of the fabric to the tracing of the edge of pattern page.

Position the assembled fuchsia unit and the bud unit over the paper pattern, matching the drawn position.

Carefully holding the fuchsia and bud in place with one hand, slide the onionskin gently out from underneath the units. To check that the units have remained in place, lay the onionskin over all pieces and compare the image shadowing through the paper with the outlines on the paper. Correct placement if necessary and remove the paper.

3. Pin the fuchsia and the bud to the background. Baste ½" from the cut edges of the large fuchsia; baste through the center of the red petals which are narrower. Baste through the center of the little bud, adding a crosswise stitch or two where the bud swells in the middle. Remove pins.

4. Appliqué the fuchsia petal #1, matching thread to the petal.

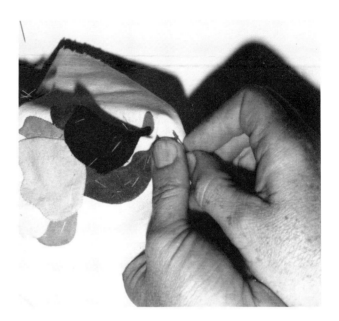

Each place where the fabric ends and another petal begins, tuck under the hem allowance of both sides of that fabric junction.

The hems will likely be folded in different directions from each other. The last stitch taken before anchoring a thread and changing color, should be taken at exactly that fabric junction. Bring the needle to the front through both fabric colors, but the thread will go over only the matching color, before returning to the back of the work.

Change thread color to appliqué each different color fabric, anchoring threads as done in the assembly.

5. After stitching petal #1, anchor and cut thread. Re-anchor it at petal #4, stitch #4 and #5. Next, appliqué #2 and #3, turning both hems at each petal junction as described.

Appliqué the dagger points of the fuchsia

Review "Appliquéing a Sampler Shape" (page 23) for illustrations of this process.

Handle the allowance of the point with the shaft of the needle rather than the tip.

Turn the green hem allowances when turning the allowance of the red pieces

The appliqué of the fuchsia and bud to the background is straightforward until you reach the top of the flowers, where the green pieces of fabric are attached by basting stitches only.

Turn the green hem allowance on both sides of the green piece as soon as it is reached in the appliqué of the red fabric; stitch the red pieces across the green. It is of no concern whether the background fabric is caught in the stitches across the green.

Return to stitch the green fabric after the red thread has been used up and anchored. At the overlap of #6 to #7, turn both fabric allowances as if they were one.

Embroider the fine detail lines

The final step in the fuchsia appliqué is to embroider the green stems above and the red stamen below the flowers.

1. Place the onionskin pattern back over the appliqué, positioning the outline over the fuchsia. Use the dent transfer to indent the lines to be embroidered

onto the background fabric. If necessary, add some length to the stems so that they continue to the edge of the background.

2. Separate the six-strand embroidery threads into individual strands. Thread a size 10 quilting needle with one strand of green.

3. Anchor the thread on the back in the background behind the green fabric of the appliqué. Begin with piece #10 or #12; both will be done the same way. Pull the needle and thread to the front of the work at the top edge of the green, precisely where it meets the background.

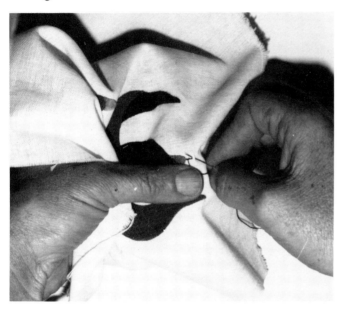

Stitch the indented stem line with ¼" long stem stitches, also called outline stitches. If necessary, refer to the glossary for the diagram of *detail stitches*. Anchor the end of the thread in the edge of the background fabric.

4. Thread the second shade of green into the needle, and embroider the same stem with another row of stem stitches, immediately against the previous row. The stem now is wider, and two-colored. Repeat this for the other stems in the design.

5. Follow the stamen embroidery lines using a single strand of the red or pink embroidery thread, with stem stitches only ⅛" long.

Alternate the shades of red for these stamen so each line appears to be closer or farther in perspective.

At the dangling end of each stamen add another three or four parallel stitches (satin stitches) for the

swelling (the anther) as drawn in the pattern. Anchor the thread behind these satin stitches.

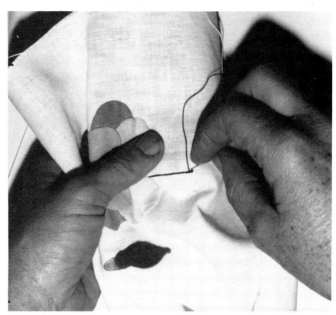

Finally, lace the needle and thread through the back of the stem stitches, not entering the fabric, for an inch before cutting the thread.

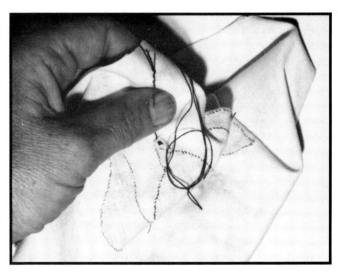

Change thread for each row of stitching, even if there is thread left from a previous row, for the embroidery thread is loosely spun and wears out quickly when stitching.

Now continue to the "Advanced Appliqué Situations and Solutions" chapter. Take special notice of the "Assembly of Units" section and learn to draw under-layer flaps. To practice the technique draft the pattern pieces for the second fuchsia, and appliqué it to the lower left-hand portion of the same background fabric.

Advanced Appliqué Situations and Solutions

Developing skills will naturally lead to the use of more challenging designs for appliqué. In the process some common situations will occur. Some of these situations will be discussed and solutions presented in this chapter. Consider the following ideas when planning an appliqué project. Rather than rules to be strictly followed, they are principles which can be used to advantage.

Using fabric grain to advantage

A large appliqué project designed for hanging on a wall or being worn as a garment will last longer and hang more smoothly if the grain line of the background fabric and the grain line of the appliqué fabric match. Artistic and construction factors will help determine whether the straight grain hangs parallel to the floor or the stretchy bias hangs parallel to the floor. Of general concern to planning the cutting of appliqué pieces is that the finished project will not twist where it is planned to be smooth. Appliqué pieces smaller than a finger may appear flat even if the grain line is not matching the background, but an appliqué larger than a business card will twist on the background fabric if grains do not match. The amount of twist will depend on how far from matching the grains are; a true bias appliquéd to a straight grain will twist more than an appliqué only slightly off grain. The twisting might be useful for special effects; let twisting be an artistic choice rather than a disappointing surprise when a piece is completed.

A carefully appliquéd project of small pieces on a background about fifteen inches square will be lightweight, and probably free of twists. If grain lines on even this small project are matched, though, there still will be one distinct advantage. The matching grain line will provide a visual reference to observe while stitching, to improve the precision of the overall finished design. Parallel to the vertical edge of the pattern, draw lines, one on each pattern piece of a design including background. Match the drawn line to the fabric grain (straight grain *or* cross grain) when positioning a pattern on fabric. Match the grain line of the appliqué pieces when positioning them on each other, and when positioning assembled units to the background. As the appliqué is stitched it is possible to unintentionally push pieces slightly out of place with the holding hand. Knowing that the pieces were cut with matching grains, creeping can immediately be corrected by realigning the grains.

Appliqué pieces cut with matching grain lines will have a visual orderliness which can camouflage stitchery techniques and emphasize the illusion of a photorealistic design. An appliqué piece cut intentionally off grain, however, can be an effective tool for communicating action. For example, if a box is falling from a table or a baseball bat is swinging at a ball, cut the fabric with the grain of the action object aimed along the direction of the action.

Marking placement on background fabrics

Placement lines can be marked, if desired, on most background fabrics by the dent transfer technique. Be sure to draw a separate pattern piece for this purpose so that the original cartoon remains intact. The technique of assembling appliqué pieces into units makes placement on the background more flexible. Simple appliqués can have units placed on the background at random. Complex appliqués can also be placed without marking the background.

Placing units of very large designs

Lay the master cartoon on the work table after all patterns have been traced. Place the pieces of your design in layers on top of the cartoon. First lay down the background. To place the units to be appliquéd directly to the background, lift the background fabric off the cartoon just enough to see the drawn location of the unit being placed. Adapt the pin-matching technique to this step, by inserting a couple of pins through the background fabric at some key corners of the unit shape showing on the cartoon. Corresponding corners of the unit being placed are then matched to the pins and basted into place.

Placing the unit onto the background without pin-matching is quite simple as well. Some background fabrics, even though they appear opaque, are translucent enough for you to see through to the cartoon. It helps if the cartoon has been outlined with very dark (and waterproof) ink. "Read" the cartoon through the fabric and carefully align each piece over the corresponding portion of the cartoon. Perfect the placement by matching the appliqué fabric grain lines with the background fabric grain line.

Placing units on small backgrounds

Placing units into specific places on small backgrounds is very easy to do. Place the assembled unit over the drawing of the unit on the cartoon. Lay the cartoon over the background fabric, positioning the cartoon so that marked grain lines match woven grain lines of the background. If the background is itself an assembled unit, feel or observe through the paper cartoon the placement of the background elements. Align the cartoon accurately with those elements. Gently hold the appliqué unit, which is in place above the cartoon, so that the unit is slightly pressed into place by your hand against the background, through the paper. With the other hand slip the paper out from between the unit and background. Perfect the placement by matching the grain lines of the background and the unit just added.

An appliqué project is small enough for this technique if it is possible for one hand to hold the unit and the other hand to slide the paper away simultaneously. If an assistant is handy, this technique will work on very large projects as long as the background is even barely visible through the cartoon paper.

Using machine-sewn seams in combination with hand appliqué

Many appliqués have portions suitable for sewing by machine. If designing such an appliqué, cut ¼" seam allowances for those areas. Mark the seams with matching-arrows every four inches on long seams, every inch on curved seams.

Underlining white and pastel fabrics

Underline white and pastel fabrics to prevent seams, hem allowances, and colors from showing through. Use a thin white or matching fabric for this type of lining. The subtle shadow from a colored underlining can be intentional; in fact shadow work is an appreciated art form in its own right. Determine whether a fabric needs an underlining. White fabric, opaque or translucent, will need underlining. Test colored fabrics by placing a white and a black fabric beside each other. Lay the color to be tested over the place the black and white meet. If the black-white change is visible through the test fabric, it needs to be underlined.

Transfer the stitching line for the appliqué piece to the underlining, matching grain lines. Cut the underlining along the stitching lines. Baste to the appliqué fabric, and treat this pair of fabrics as one. Embroidery on the appliqué should be stitched through the underlining at the same time. The threads beneath the embroidered fabric will be hidden by the underlining and the fabric will have more body to support the embroidery. Plan to leave the background fabric intact when the appliqué is completed, rather than trimming the fabric away behind the design. Underlinings are not usually caught in the appliqué stitching, and removing the background layer of fabric will cause the underlining to shift or fall away from the appliqué, defeating its purpose.

Assembling units: under-layer flaps

A design which first seemed simple may prove complicated by the time it is drawn. Assembly can be simplified by separating the design into small units. Assemble separate units, then join to other units or to the background. The background may be composed of different pieces, in which case cut and assemble background pieces as one unit.

A complicated design, 10" x 9"

Cut and assemble each unit separately. Where individual units overlap each other in the final plan, join those individual units into a larger unit. Once all units are completed experiment with the placement of units on the background until all elements of the design are positioned to satisfaction. Baste and appliqué units in place.

Wherever one fabric overlaps and will be stitched to another, the underneath fabric needs an extra-large allowance cut beyond the matching stitching line. This allowance is called an under-layer flap.

Analyze each piece of the design to determine which needs an under-layer flap or two and which does not. For example, perhaps a hat doesn't need a flap, but the hair sticking out below the hat will. The head under the hair will need a flap where the hair joins it; the neck will need a flap where the chin joins, *as well as* one where the shirt joins.

Each under-layer flap should be large enough to hold basting stitches, and large enough to be grasped in the holding fingers. The best general guideline is to draw and cut under-layers as large as your thumbprint. Even small appliqué pieces can be handled easily as long as the flap is generous. Extra fabric can be trimmed away after the appliqué has been stitched to the flap.

Large appliqué pieces should have under-layer flaps wider than your thumb. The objective is to have plenty of fabric to hold onto while appliquéing the piece, so that you have control.

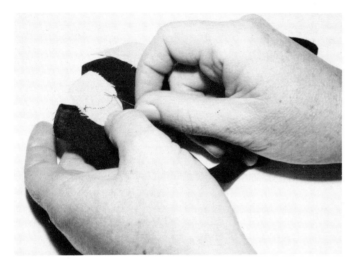

The under-layer flap must be large enough to baste the top layer to. It must fit solidly in the fingers while stitching.

The flap may need to be larger than the piece which is being stitched to it.

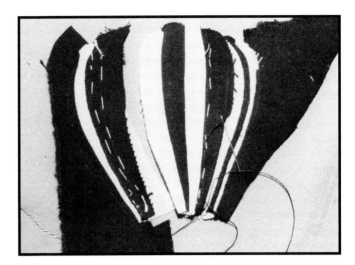

Be generous. Fabric can be trimmed after stitching is completed.

Sometimes an appliqué layer can be padded with the under-layer flap. For example, use the head flap to fill out the hair layer, making it appear thicker.

Draw the appliqué pattern piece with all stitching lines, including the one to which the overlapping fabric will be stitched. That is the matching-line. For visual reference, draw the under-layer flap outline with a *dotted* or broken line. As the flap meets the matching line, it must continue beyond the appliqué stitching line to become the ⅛" hem allowance. It is not necessary to draw the entire hem allowance cutting line, but do draw the first ¼" section of the hem allowance beyond the matching line.

Switching layers of fabric mid-line

A fabric may need to switch layers in an appliqué design. The design may call for hair to be stitched to a girl's forehead, then tucked behind her ear. If that ear is cut as part of the face appliqué piece, the face fabric changes position from the underneath layer and becomes the overlay. To accomplish this, clip the hair hem allowance to the stitching line where it will meet the ear stitching line. Butt the folded edge of the ear against the clipped corner and appliqué the ear to the hair.

Adding detail

The most effective way to add delicate details like facial features, eyelashes and fingernails is with embroidery. Some subtle details such as fabric folds can be quilted into the finished appliqué. Plan either type of detailing on the paper pattern. Transfer detailing lines to the fabric when transferring stitching lines.

To add details, use embroidery floss for fill-in areas of stitches only. It is a loosely twisted thread which comes in a six-strand skein and hundreds of colors. It is the best thread for fill-in stitching, giving a soft feathery appearance. To keep embroidery in scale with the delicate appliqué, embroider stitches with a single strand of floss. For areas where a fine line is to be embroidered, sewing thread is a better choice. The tighter twist of the sewing thread gives single strand embroidery a firm quality and precise appearance. Sewing thread is not the choice for most fill-in areas since each stitch will stand out distinctly, but there will be instances where that effect would provide the desired texture.

Some appliqué pieces will receive many embroidery stitches. When appliquéing the baseball batter uniform from the pattern section of this book, observe that the shirt of the uniform is embroidered with the team logo. When you are going to embroider fabric pieces, cut them with a very wide allowance beyond the intended hem allowance. Baste a properly-cut (along stitching lines) underlining to the shirt if the appliqué fabric needs one. Embroider the fabrics as if they were one, first outlining the letters with sewing thread then filling-in the areas with single strand embroidery floss stitches. When the embroidery is complete, recut the appliqué pattern piece with the ⅛" hem allowance and the under-layer flap at the waist. The larger rough cut allows for the extra handling of embroidery without any fraying of the hem allowance of the appliqué.

Where there is an abundance of embroidered detail, embroider on the marked but rough-cut fabric.

Some embroidery must be done after the assembled unit has been stitched to the background fabric.

If embroidery outlines a fabric edge or continues beyond it, those lines must be embroidered after the appliqué is completed.

Photo-realistic appliqués owe much of their success to their delicate treatment of detail. On a pictorial appliqué, particularly one featuring people, use simple stitches which won't draw attention to themselves. Here are some effective stitches:

wide lines: closely worked fly stitches, chain stitches
bold yet narrow lines: stem stitches (also called outline stitches)
delicate narrow lines: backstitches
broken lines: running stitches
dotted lines: seed stitches

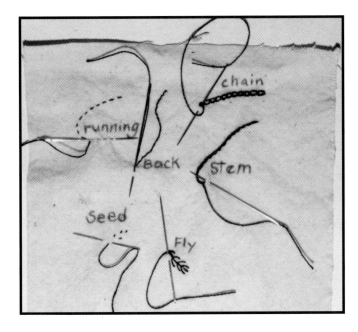

Fill-in areas of embroidery will use the same selection of stitches, in rows close together. When filling in an area with multiple rows of stitches, narrow the embroidery line where necessary by switching, mid-row, to another kind of stitch. Any line of embroidery can start with one type of stitch and evolve into narrower or wider types of stitches as the designer chooses. The calligraphic quality of such an evolving row of stitches will add an illusion of perspective.

Trimming away back layers

Some quilters carefully trim away the hidden layers of their work to reduce bulk when they quilt. If this is your intention, plan ahead. Take anchor stitches close to stitching lines and trim well past all stitches. Leave hidden layers intact behind appliqué pieces which have been underlined.

Making hand appliquéd garments

Preshrink all fabrics to be used in an appliquéd garment project.

When designing a garment that will be appliquéd, cut a duplicate set of pattern pieces for all sections of the garment to be embellished. Duplicates can be made on pattern paper, non-woven pattern fabric or blank newsprint. The fashion fabric will be cut from the original pattern pieces.

Appliqué designs will be positioned and drawn on the duplicates and then either traced to onionskin paper or transferred directly to the appliqué fabric. Label duplicate pattern pieces to indicate the right and wrong side of garment, front, back and left or right sleeve. Include markings for darts, seam allowances, hems, grain lines, pockets and other intended construction details.

Planning appliqué to flatter the body

If using an unfamiliar pattern, make a "muslin" of the garment before cutting the pattern duplicates. A muslin is a sample made of any inexpensive fabric but preferably one which drapes the way the fashion fabric will. For example, if the appliquéd garment will be a slinky silk fabric, a sample actually made of muslin fabric, although showing whether the pattern measurements are correct, won't indicate whether the garment will move with the body gracefully.

A muslin is usually cut with extra-wide seam allowances and sewn inside out. Alterations are drawn on the fabric and seams opened, if necessary, while the sample is being modeled by the person for whom it is being made. While the muslin is on the body, mark it, noting where the most flattering areas are for placing the appliqué designs. Note where appliqué details would be "wasted" (hidden under an arm, hidden under hair) or be unflattering (does this particular body look great with an appliqué at the bust or the waistline?).

If alterations have been made to the pattern, the altered pattern pieces are the ones to duplicate.

Should this be a pattern already tried and proven successful, it is still a wise idea to model the garment to observe the most flattering locations for decorating with appliqué. Note these observations on the duplicate pattern pieces.

The fabric chosen for the appliqué fabric will help determine the size of the shapes to be designed for a project. Fine weave fabrics can be appliquéd in small and complex shapes. Heavier fabrics need larger scale designs. If the appliqué fabric requires a wide hem allowance, then it needs wide shapes in the appliqué design. The hem allowances needed for the appliqué depend on the character of the appliqué fabric, not the garment fabric. Fabrics woven with many threads per inch (50 or more) need ⅛" hem allowances. Coarser fabrics with fewer threads per inch (corduroy, velveteen, homespun) need ¼" hem allowances. Allowances of ¼" turned from both sides of a thin corduroy stem will fit if the stem is at least ⅜" wide. Due to the scale of the whole garment in that fabric, the ⅜" stem will appear to be narrow.

The appliqué pattern

When it is clear, from the fitted pattern pieces and selected fabric, what size to design the appliqué patterns, sketch some design ideas on paper other than the pattern duplicates. When a design is refined into a desired appliqué, position it under the duplicate pattern pieces and trace it in place. Blank newsprint is more opaque than pattern paper, so if that is the substance of the duplicate, the design to be traced should be drawn with a very dark ink or taped in place under the duplicate and drawn while it is held against a window during daylight or a light table. Draw the grain line on the appliqué design, extending or paralleling the one which was previously copied on the duplicate.

Try the dent transfer on a scrap of the selected appliqué fabric. If the indentation shows on the fabric, then transfer the designs directly from the duplicate pattern pieces. The designs should be positioned so that the grain line of the appliqué matches the grain line of the garment section it is stitched to. Use a finger tip to crease a half inch of grain line on the pattern and lift part of the pattern from the fabric so the crease can be matched with a thread of the weave.

Some fabrics will not show the indentation. To transfer the design to those fabrics, trace the design on non-woven pattern fabric or non-woven interfacing. Paper can be substituted if the non-woven interfacing materials are not available. For a template, cut the appliqué design from the tracing, including the hem allowance needed outside the stitching lines. Pin, baste or hold the cut template to the appliqué fabric, matching the drawn grain line to the fabric grain line. Cut the appliqué around the template, first with a small rotary cutter, then use small sharp scissors to fine tune the cutting line. See page 17 for another method which involves indenting muslin.

Pre-assembling the garment or garment sections

Parts of the garment may need some assembly before the appliqué is added. Sew darts and stay stitch curved and bias edges.

Multilayer reverse appliqué vests may need to be sewn before you mark, cut and stitch the appliqué. Leave a six-inch opening at the hem and do not sew the shoulder seams, so the vest can be turned right side out. This step is for vests which will be lined and finished without facings at the openings. The multiple fabric layers sewn into the armhole, neck, front and bottom seams will function as interfacings, providing the stability needed at the openings for the vest to hold its shape when worn.

When the design will be appliquéd over garment seams, stitch that part of the appliqué after the seam has been sewn, even if most of the appliqué is stitched before the seams are sewn.

Appliqué designs which will "float" in the garment section, not interacting with garment seams at all, are easiest to appliqué before any seams are sewn. Cut the garment section, stitch any darts in the section, stay stitch and if possible, overlock (serge or zigzag) the fabric edges. Then cut, baste and stitch the appliqué on the fashion fabric.

Positioning and appliquéing the design

Position the appliqués on the garment pieces, following the plans drawn on the duplicate patterns. Baste and appliqué the design, as learned in the previous sections of this book. Most garments are handled, worn, washed or cleaned and hung or folded. They need to be durable throughout this use. When appliquéing, make sure stitches are close and tight. Fabrics needing ¼" hem allowance will be strong with eight stitches per inch as long as the stitches are snugly pulled into the folded edge of the fabric. Lighterweight, finely woven fabrics with ⅛" hem allowance should be appliquéd with 20 stitches per inch. Especially finely woven fabrics, should they be used, may need 30 or 40 stitches per inch, but then the hem allowances could be as delicate as ¹⁄₁₆" or ¹⁄₂₀". An example of this type would be appliquéing design elements cut of china silk, which has such a fine weave that the stitches barely nick the folded edge of fabric and need to be exceptionally close together if they are to be invisible as well as durable.

Slippery fabric usually requires that more than three anchor stitches be taken to begin and end stitching lines. Test the anchor stitches after three are taken. Does the thread stay anchored? If not, try four stitches and test. Once it is determined how many stitches are needed, that is the formula to be followed every time that fabric is appliquéd.

Baseball Batter:
An Advanced Appliqué Project

The author extends sincere thanks to Mr. Patrick J. Gallagher and the San Francisco Giants for allowing use of the Giants logo in this pattern.

Pattern pieces for the ball player

Although pattern pieces are provided for this project, it is recommended that you draft your own patterns as an exercise. Build confidence through practice. Trace each pattern piece for the batter from the master cartoon to onionskin paper, drafting under-layer flaps where necessary. Trace embroidery and grain lines. After drafting the pattern pieces, compare them to those provided on page 63, to check for accuracy of under-layers.

Drafting the pattern for the Baseball Batter

The cartoon and pattern pieces for this project can be found on pages 62 and 63.

1. Trace the entire picture for the master cartoon. It is easiest to create this appliqué in a slightly larger size. I recommend, if you are approaching the pattern at all timidly, that you find a photocopy machine which will allow you to increase the size to 143% of its printed size. Mark fabric grain lines (parallel to the edges of the cartoon's outside box) through each portion of the cartoon.

2. On a sheet of onionskin paper, use a ruler to draw the following rectangles:

for the 143% baseball batter:

    a. 15" x 4" for the **sand**
    b. 15" x 1¼" for the **grass**
    c. 15" x 11" for the **far background wall**

for the actual size baseball batter:

    a. 11" x 2¼" for the **sand**
    b. 11" x 1" for the **grass**
    c. 11" x 6¼" for the **far background wall**

These rectangles include ¾" allowances on all outside edges for trimming or adding a border and ¼" allowances for stitching the rectangles together.

Use the straight edges of the rectangles to match grain lines; add matching-arrows for the longest edges, if desired, for use in joining the rectangles.

From the master cartoon drawn in step one:

3. Trace to onionskin the **front crowd** (lower) section, adding ¾" allowances on each side for ease of handling. Add an extra ¼" allowance at the bottom edge for stitching it to the grass rectangle.

4. Repeat for the **back (upper) crowd** section. Use the upper **grass** line for the bottom stitching line of **back crowd** and add ¼" seam allowance.

This small appliqué uses only a few color repeats. Arrange fabrics before beginning to cut and sew. Use colors that work well for you. Coloring the drawing may help you visualize the color scheme. (See the color reproduction of the sample, page 78).

Color suggestions for the baseball batter:

    Light gray - **far wall**
    Medium gray - **back row of the crowd**
    Blue-gray - **front row of the crowd**
    White - **socks**, body of **uniform** (underline)
    Pale cream - **back leg** (underline with white)
    Black - batter's **gloves, helmet** and **shoes**
    Green - **grass** behind batter's legs
    Tan - **sand** under batter's feet
    Your choice of **skin** color (underline translucent)
    Beige wood color - **bat**

Color suggestions for the embroidery:

    Black thread – **bat tip** line, **uniform creases, face, stripes**, and **logo** on shirt
    Orange – **uniform stripes** and "Giants" **logo**
    White – **glove, shoe, helmet** details

Select *sewing thread* to embroider each outline and single-line detail. Select matching *embroidery floss* to fill in the outlined logo, uniform stripes and shoe design areas.

Assembling the background unit

1. Transfer the pattern to fabric. Cut rectangles as drawn because seam allowances are included in the pattern.

Matching-arrows can be marked in the *allowances*.

2. Cut the **crowd sections**. Allow a ⅛" hem for the upper edges of the **crowd** sections which will be appliquéd. Clip *inside curves* and *inside corners*. Use either of the following methods to join the background unit:

Method One:

3. Set your sewing machine stitch length at 15 stitches per inch; stitch the **sand** to the **grass** (with a ¼" seam).

4. Match the *lower edges* of the light-gray **back wall** and the two **crowd sections**. Stitch these three edges as one piece to the **grass**.

5. Grade these seam allowances to reduce bulk, for instance one at ⅛", one at 1/16", one at 3/16". Press seams toward the **sand** section.

6. Baste and appliqué the *upper edges* of the **crowd sections**.

Note where the **batter unit** will eventually be stitched over these pieces. Reduce the seam bulk "behind the batter" by tapering the *hem allowances* of the upper edge of the **crowd section** to nothing.

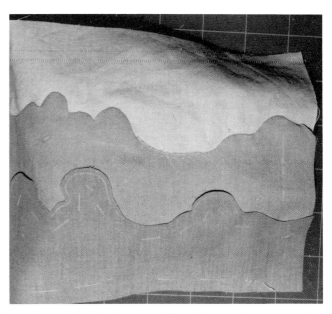

As you appliqué, stop appliquéing and use running stitches to tack this area down; then begin to appliqué again ¼" from where the batter fabric will end.

Turn at least a ¼" segment of the **crowd section** fabric "behind the batter" at each side to allow a margin for error.

Method Two:

3. Match the *bottom edges* of the **back wall** and **top crowd section**. Baste ½" from *all edges*.

Appliqué the **back crowd** to the **back wall**. Remove basting stitches.

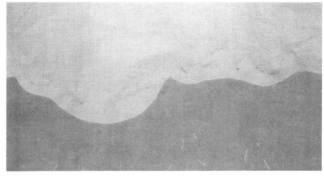

Trim the **back wall** under-layer to ¼" following the appliqué line.

4. Baste and appliqué **front crowd** in the same way. Trim **back crowd** under-layer.

5. Hand or machine stitch **front crowd** to **grass** and **grass** to **sand**, as in Method One.

6. Press seams toward **sand** section. Trim as needed to reduce bulk.

NOTE: the appliqué stitches should begin and end ½" from side edges of the piece. This allows ¼" to be stitched in the side seam allowance and leaves ½" unstitched for trimming allowances after the appliqué is complete.

Assembling the ball player unit

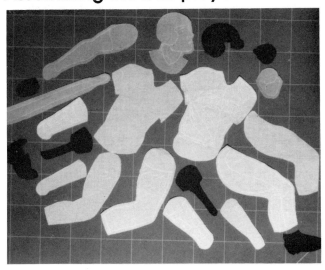

1. Transfer and cut all pieces of the **batter.** Cut hem allowances ¹⁄₁₂" from stitching lines. Transfer *all embroidery lines* but not grain lines. Transfer and cut **underlinings.**

Cut hem allowances for under-layer flaps ⅛" beyond stitching lines, angling the allowance to nothing (see sample drafted pattern pieces).

2. Lay fabric pieces on top of each other as they will appear when appliquéd. Slip a slick postcard or paper underneath this assembly of pieces and then slip them, intact, onto the background unit.

Do the colors work together in the picture? Walk across the room to get another perspective. This is the time to change a color and cut a new fabric piece if you think another arrangement might look better.

When the results are satisfactory, return batter assembly to work table.

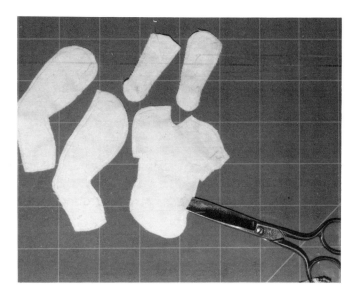

3. Baste underlinings in place, ¼" from cut edges of the underlinings.

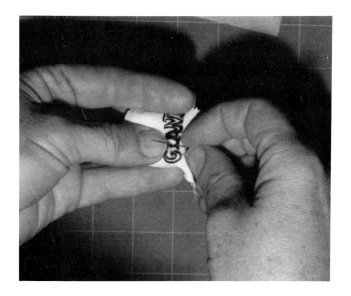

4. Embroider the team logo on the **shirt** with a single strand of black embroidery floss, **using stem and chain** stitches. Outline the logo with **stem stitches** in orange sewing thread.

Use the pin-matching technique to align the stitching-lines where they form corners on an appliqué piece with the matching-lines where they form corners with stitching lines on the under-layer. Matching-arrows are only on pattern pieces where no corners are formed by adjoining stitching lines.

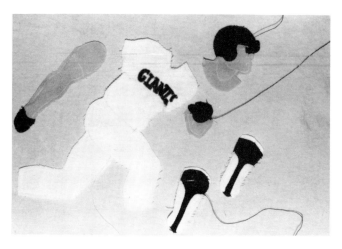

5. Baste and appliqué the pieces in pairs: **stirrup** to **sock**, **glove** to **arm**, **helmet** to **head**, **trouser legs** to each other, and **shirt** to **trousers.**

In the photo above, notice that some of the threads were left attached to short stitching lines, after the anchor stitches were taken to secure the hem. These threads can be used to stitch the pieces to the background when the batter unit is complete.

The tiny helmet-brim can be butted up against the forehead after the forehead is attached to the background fabric.

The under-layer flaps for the socks and the stirrups were graded to different widths to reduce bulk.

6. Baste and appliqué the **shoes** to **socks**, **head** to **shirt**, **arms** to **shirt** and **bat** to **glove**.

46

7. Baste and appliqué the **socks** to the **trousers**.

8. Working from the back of the assembled **batter**, use only the *tip* of a steam iron to gently steam press along *stitching lines*. Turn the appliqué so the front of the work faces you. Hold the iron flat so it is hovering just above the surface of the appliqué. Steam the piece. While the fabric is still steamy, finger-press lightly with clean fingers.

9. Trim any under-layers which are too bulky or will interfere with turning hem allowances. Some under-layers might remain for padding.

10. Place the **batter unit** on the **background unit**, covering unstitched sections of the crowd. If more precise placement is desired: place the **batter unit** on the master cartoon, aligning all elements of the design; then place the paper cartoon over the **background unit**, feeling or noticing where the drawn crowd characters align with the fabric characters. Lightly hold the **batter unit** to the paper with one hand, with the other hand, slip the paper out from between the fabric layers. If fabric grain lines have been matched during the assembly process, all batter grain lines should be aligned with the grain line of the background. Baste the **batter** in place.

If thread was left dangling after anchoring the short stitching lines, thread it into the needle where you encounter it, as you appliqué batter to background. Otherwise, anchor matching thread to each change in fabric color.

11. Begin to appliqué at the head, as it is the layer closest to the background. Stitch the lower layers of fabric first, then the upper layers.

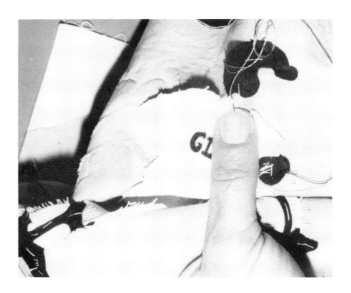

At the back of the **neck** (skin color), tuck just enough of the **shoulder** hem (white uniform) to catch its edge in the corner stitch at neck. Do this step wherever two fabrics join and will be turned in different directions.

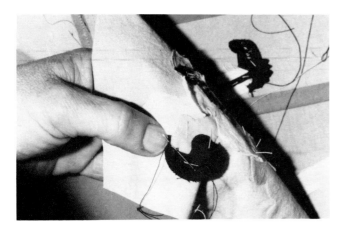

Stitch the helmet-brim to the forehead as soon as the forehead is stitched to the background. Butt the folded edges together.

Proceed to the arms, socks and bat. Appliqué each layer of fabric, changing thread color to match.

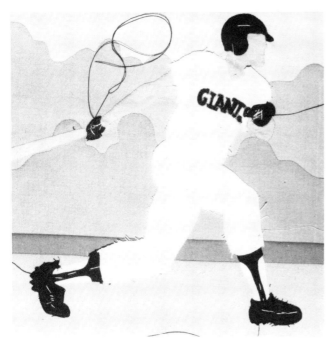

Head, helmet, arms, socks and bat are finished. Now the back glove is being appliquéd.

Back of uniform, back of rear leg and socks are finished. Now the front of the rear leg is being appliquéd.

Appliqué the shoes and raised glove last. When all pieces have been sewn, remove the basting stitches.

The finished appliqué.

The appliqué with the embroidered details.

Embroidering the details

Satin stitch the **cheek patches**; chain stitch the **logo on the helmet**; use stem stitches and detached satin stitches on the **ear section of helmet**. Backstitch to define **brim**; use running stitches for the **under brim** and stem stitch the **glove**.

The stitches on *steps 1-6* are all to be done with *single strand sewing thread*. See the beginning of the chapter for color suggestions for embroidery.

1. Embroider stem stitches on the **chin outline** and **eyebrows**. Make the **eyebrow** two rows wide at the temple and three rows by the nose.

2. Define the **eyelid** with tiny running stitches.

3. Embroider the **eye** with three satin stitches. Satin stitches are backstitches placed closely beside each other rather than in a row.

4. Stitch the **nose line** from brow to tip with running stitches. Backstitch the **nostril**; use a stem stitch on the **nostril hole**.

5. Do stem stitches for the **mouth.**

6. Use *brown* thread to satin stitch the **dark cheek patches under the eyes.**

7. Stem stitch the **stripes at the hem of the sleeve** with single strand embroidery thread.

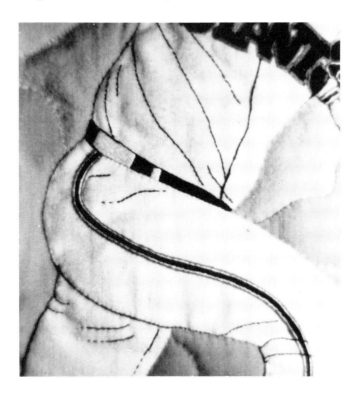

8. Use single strand of sewing thread to embroider *individual lines* of backstitches, stem stitches and running stitches. Make the **fold lines** in the uniform of varying boldness. Use single strand embroidery thread to stem stitch rows for the **leg stripes**; embroider the **belt** with black and the **belt loops** with white, using

multiple rows of stem stitches.

9. Use a single strand of sewing thread to stem stitch the **center-front shirt line**, the outline at **cuff of the sleeve, the fingers on gloves** and the **outline separating legs.**

10. Single strands of embroidery thread are used in stem and chain stitches to decorate the **shoes**, and in satin stitches at the **upper back of the heel.** Sewing thread is needed to define the **stirrups** and **heel soles** with running stitches; work fly and chain stitches for the **shoelaces.**

11. To accent the **bat**, outline the lower edge in black sewing thread with running stitches.

12. Stem stitch the **shadow on the sand** with single strand embroidery floss.

After completing the embroidery work, this appliqué is finished. Trim edges to square the block. Add a border if desired. Pin the appliqué to a curtain or a flannel-covered board, somehow displaying the piece so that you can now step across the room to admire it from a distance.

Having completed this appliqué sample, you should feel confident enough to embark on any appliqué project. You have learned the essential techniques.

Designing for appliqué

Having practiced some basic appliqué, you are now ready to design.

Sources for design

1. Photographs are great design tools. Although you can never copy a photograph exactly with appliqué, you can catch the essence of the scene. Photographs help create a facsimile of life.

2. Develop many beautiful and intricate designs from your imagination. Use original sketches. Geometric or free-flowing shapes transfer easily into an appliqué.

3. Carry a sketch book. Draw anything that excites the imagination—landscapes, children, buildings. The sketch book will soon be full of ideas needing only to be refined. Even stick figures can convey a sense of action or direction, a quick mental snapshot of a mood. When taking photographs, make a quick sketch as well. There are gestures and moods that the camera can't catch. These gestures and moods give character to the work.

Trust yourself. No artist could produce treasures without first practicing the craft. Here the quality of the drawing is not important. Experiment. Have fun with color and shapes. Allow yourself freedom; you may create some exceptional designs.

Planning a pattern

The simplest appliqué would consist of one piece of fabric placed at random on a background. A more complicated design may include geometric images. Geometric designs may be symmetrical or asymmetrical. If your design is a pictorial appliqué, the image will be more dynamic if the focus of attention is deliberately off-center.

Plan layers so important features will not interfere with each other.

A distant tree would look better placed behind or in front of the boy's head rather than growing out of the top. The line of a mountain ridge would look better placed behind his head, about eyebrow height, or rising above his head, rather than crossing exactly at the top hairline.

Once sketching is finished, the design may be enlarged by one of the methods discussed earlier. Draw enlargements with a relaxed hand. Whether done with a smooth or a sketchy line, some of the pattern may need to be refined once it has been enlarged. How much time you need to spend re-drawing will depend on the subject and on how much detail is desired.

Add details from your imagination or use a magnifying tool to study the details in the photo. When re-creating a scene, sometimes a detail will need to be traced from the photograph to be precise. Whichever method is used, time should be spent on the drawing stages to complete the picture. Guesswork on details will be frustrating later when you're beginning to sew.

When the design is complete, draw over the lines with dark, waterproof ink. Do not cut the drawing apart. This is the original "cartoon" that will help determine the placement of the appliqué. From this cartoon, trace individual paper patterns for cutting the fabric.

Generally, the grain line of the appliqué runs perpendicular to the bottom of the pattern. Draw the grainlines through each piece of the cartoon. Be sure these lines are bold. Trace them when tracing the paper pattern pieces.

Machine-joined seams should have matching-arrows placed in the seam allowances. Draw at least two arrows for each seam. If the seam is longer than four or five inches, more arrows will be useful.

Newsprint works well for tracing large background pieces. When the cartoon is drawn with dark lines, those lines are quite visible through unprinted newsprint. Use onionskin typing paper where possible for pattern pieces. Take care to trace each shape, each color change and any detail lines. Draw under-layer flaps as described in the Assembly of Units section of the "Advanced Appliqué" chapter.

Designing with photographs

Projectors are useful to designers developing large sketches from photographs. Greatly enlarged photographs lack the crisp details seen in the small photo being enlarged, but the proportions and important outlines are available for drawing. Slides should be projected on paper fixed to a smooth wall (slide projection screens move when touched, are delicate and are textured). Use any slide projector to enlarge the slides. Opaque projectors will enlarge or reduce the size of printed material: sketches, photographs, magazine pictures. Some opaque projectors effectively project an image from three-dimensional objects. Each model of opaque projector will have a different place to put the photograph, and will have a different limit to the size of the photo which can be reflected by the mirrors inside. Art stores sell opaque projectors; some will rent time for in-store use of a projector owned by the store. Equipment and party supply rental shops often have opaque projectors for rent. Some of the small projectors are advertised for sale in sewing magazines; by contacting the company, you may find that larger projectors are also available. Some large projectors available have the ability to project images on a table surface as well as on a wall.

Project the photograph to the drawing paper. A darkened room is essential for seeing the image clearly. Maximum darkness will reveal maximum clarity, but a drawing can be done during daylight hours by blocking light from windows. The image will contain more information than is necessary for an appliqué pattern. Simplify the picture you draw by selecting the important features from the image. What are the lines which tell the story? Which details convey the shape of the forms? Which shadows really add to the story? Which interfere? Some shadows on people look more like birthmarks once they are appliquéd. Draw the lines selected.

The original photograph will project most clearly if there is strong contrast between the design elements to be copied and the background elements. If the distinction between subject and background is not clear, it may be easier to first trace the important lines from the photo on transparent tracing paper. Enlarge the tracing. In some cases it may be necessary to draw directly on the photograph with black ink to get a definite outline before tracing. If you do not have a pen which will draw successfully on a photo, inquire at a camera shop about a pen designed for the purpose (this should cost no more than any other pen).

Before moving the drawing or the projector, either stand in front of the light from the projector, shine a flashlight on the drawing in progress, or turn a room light on, to see if any lines have been incompletely drawn.

For small projects, a photograph can be enlarged at a photo lab to the size of the appliqué pattern. A 16" x 20" enlargement can be expensive, but an 8" x 10" or 8" x 12" is about the price of a roll of film. Use transparent tracing paper to draw directly over the photograph, remembering to select the important information and leave out the other details.

Techniques for drafting patterns from these drawings are discussed in the "Baseball Batter: An Advanced Appliqué Project" chapter (page 43). Study the drafted patterns in the pattern section (page 56) to help analyze the under-layer flaps for your own design.

Trouble-Shooting

Q - Do your appliqué stitches look like little beads on the folded edge?

1. Pull each stitch tighter when stitching, not enough to pucker the edge, but enough to sink the stitch into the weave.

2. Check to make sure only two or three threads of fabric are being taken in each stitch.

Q - Do the curves in hemmed edges appear to have small flat sections when they should be smooth?

1. Stitches may be too far apart.

2. Clips may be too far apart.

3. Clips may be too deep into the hem allowance.

4. A clip may need to be deeper into the hem allowance, even as little as one thread deeper.

5. Use more care when turning the edge under with the needle tip or needle shaft.

You can correct the line to a certain degree by sliding the needle tip between the fabric layers and carefully adjusting the hem allowance so that it lies more smoothly. Slide the needle between the appliqué and hem allowance, and use the tip of the needle to pull the folded edge in or poke it out slightly from inside.

Q - Are the seams underneath the finished appliqué bulky ?

1. Grade the under-layer flaps more when they are trimmed.

2. Perhaps too many seams intersect. Grade hem allowances from the back of the work, taking care not to trim them narrower than $1/12$", as they might pull out. All stitching should remain intact.

3. Perhaps layers which could have been left un-stitched were turned and stitched between the appliqué and the background.

Q - Are edges raveling or poking out from under the fold?

1. The edge needs more stitches per inch. Go back and add stitches or rip out the original hem and re-stitch.

2. If only one vagrant thread pokes out of an otherwise secure hem, take a stitch directly on top of the jutting thread to trap it against the hem fold.

3. It may be necessary to take a deeper hem.

4. In the case of an inside curve or inside corner, the hem needs to be rolled more firmly past the stitching line to fold past the clips.

Q - Is an outside corner so narrow that some threads are unraveling from the point?

1. Was the point stitched with the thinnest possible needle?

2. Add enough extra stitches so the edge is almost re-woven. It is better to take a greater number of tiny stitches rather than fewer longer ones.

3. Be sure the sides of the point are trimmed to a narrow ($1/12$") tapered hem allowance; the $1/8$" long tip is not cut squarely, but slightly rounded.

4. Try to fold the tip of the hem allowance under the tip of the point in a smooth sweep which resembles the action of the second-hand of a clock. The allowance should move in a single sweep to point in the exact opposite direction than it started in. Practice this action on some scraps to develop the touch, and soon points will turn perfectly on the first attempt.

5. Be sure the stitches catch the folded edge of the upper fabric layer but none of the folded edge of the inside, hem allowance layers.

Q - Does the fabric edge want to ravel as the hem allowance is tucked under with the needle tip?

1. Fabric grain will affect the behavior of cut edges. Tuck with the shaft of the needle from the other direction (toward last stitches taken or away from stitches taken) if the first attempt to turn the hem allowance isn't smooth.

Raw edges will either tuck smoothly or they will resist and fray. If they resist, simply tuck them from the other direction.

Q - Did your appliqué pieces end up askew after stitching?

1. More basting may be necessary.

2. Match grain lines for all pieces as you baste them together and keep them matched as you appliqué.

Q - Is the end product slightly rippled?

1. Take more care to match grain lines during appliqué.

2. When stitches are pulled snugly they are locked by the perpendicular shape at the hem fold. If they appear gathered, it is likely that the stitches are either diagonal both in front and behind the fabric, or that they are being taken more parallel to the fold than needed.

3. The finished appliqué can be salvaged by backing the appliqué with batting and fabric, then quilting.

Q - Do the outside curves fray?

1. This will happen if outside curves are mistakenly clipped.

2. The hem allowance may need to be wider.

Q - Is there one loose stitch in the middle of a stitching line?

1. Anchor a new thread *behind* the appliqué near the loose stitch, but as far away as the loop is long. Slide your needle through the loop of the loose stitch, hooking it with the new thread. Pull the loop tight, then anchor the new thread again.

Q - Does the stitching line have one poorly executed section?

1. Snip the thread at the problem area and pick out stitches for about an inch in each direction from the snip. Anchor those short ends of thread by inserting a *threadless* needle into the background fabric far enough that only the eye is visible. Thread the eye with the inch of thread, pull thread through the fabric. Repeat until the thread ends are anchored. Re-stitch the problem area.

Q - Does the thread knot and break during sewing?

1. Appliqué wears thread out quickly because so many small stitches are taken per inch of thread. Cut each thread no longer than 18". Replace thread as it shows signs of wear. Begin each new section of appliqué with a new length of thread.

2. Knots are often formed by twisting thread. Untwist the thread by dangling the threaded needle in the air. The needle will rotate and untwist the thread.

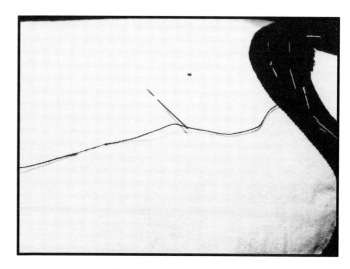

A thread longer than 18" will wear out before its end is reached.

Patterns

These patterns can provide practice in various skills. Some cartoons have all the pattern pieces drafted (complete with under-layer flaps) for tracing. For some designs, after tracing the cartoon and main pattern pieces, it will be necessary to draft background patterns.

Some designs are presented as master cartoons only, and all pattern pieces must be drafted. Whether or not you wish to stitch those designs, they are still valuable as pattern drafting exercises. Principles for drafting under-layer flaps are discussed in the chapter: "Advanced Appliqué Situations and Solutions" (page 36).

Extend background fabrics "beyond the page" so there is an allowance for trimming the edges of the finished project and so that seam allowances will be included for finishing with a border if desired. If backgrounds are machine-pieced (the cat on the windowsill, the tricycle rider, the baseball batter), press the seams to one side. Do not press the seams open.

Embroider thin-line details such as the fishing rod and line, hummingbird beak and fuchsia stamen. Some details can be quilted in place; quilt the outer edges of the appliqué units "in the ditch" to add more dimension.

After mastering the patterns in this section, design your own appliqué projects. Your pride in workmanship will soar when you can say, "I designed this myself."

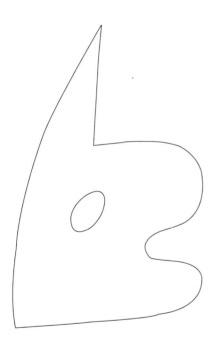

SAMPLER SHAPE
for use with
"Appliquéing a Sampler Shape"
(page 19)

Clipping guide for eye

Clipping guide for mouth

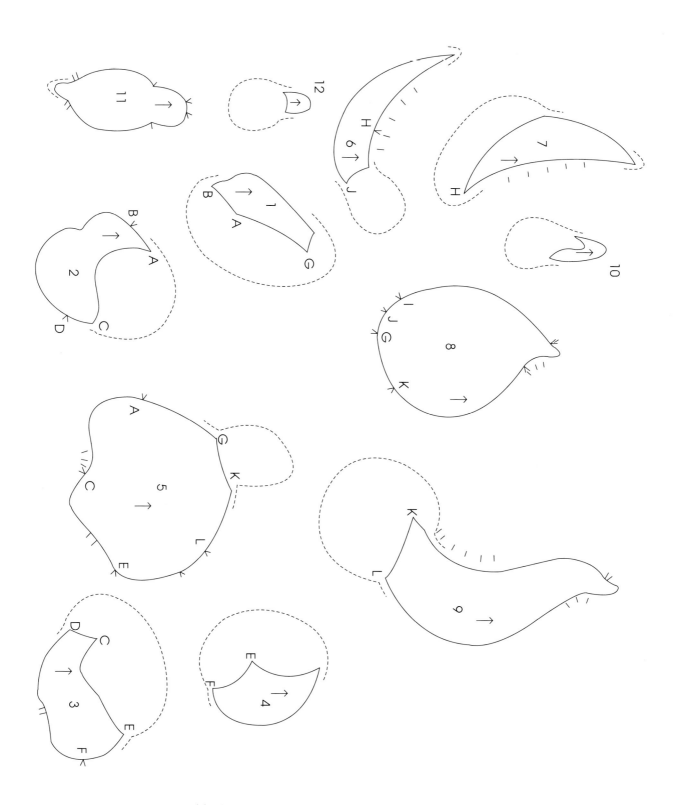

V - shaped marks are matching arrows
| - shaped marks are clipping guide marks
---- are cutting line guides and under-layer flaps

59

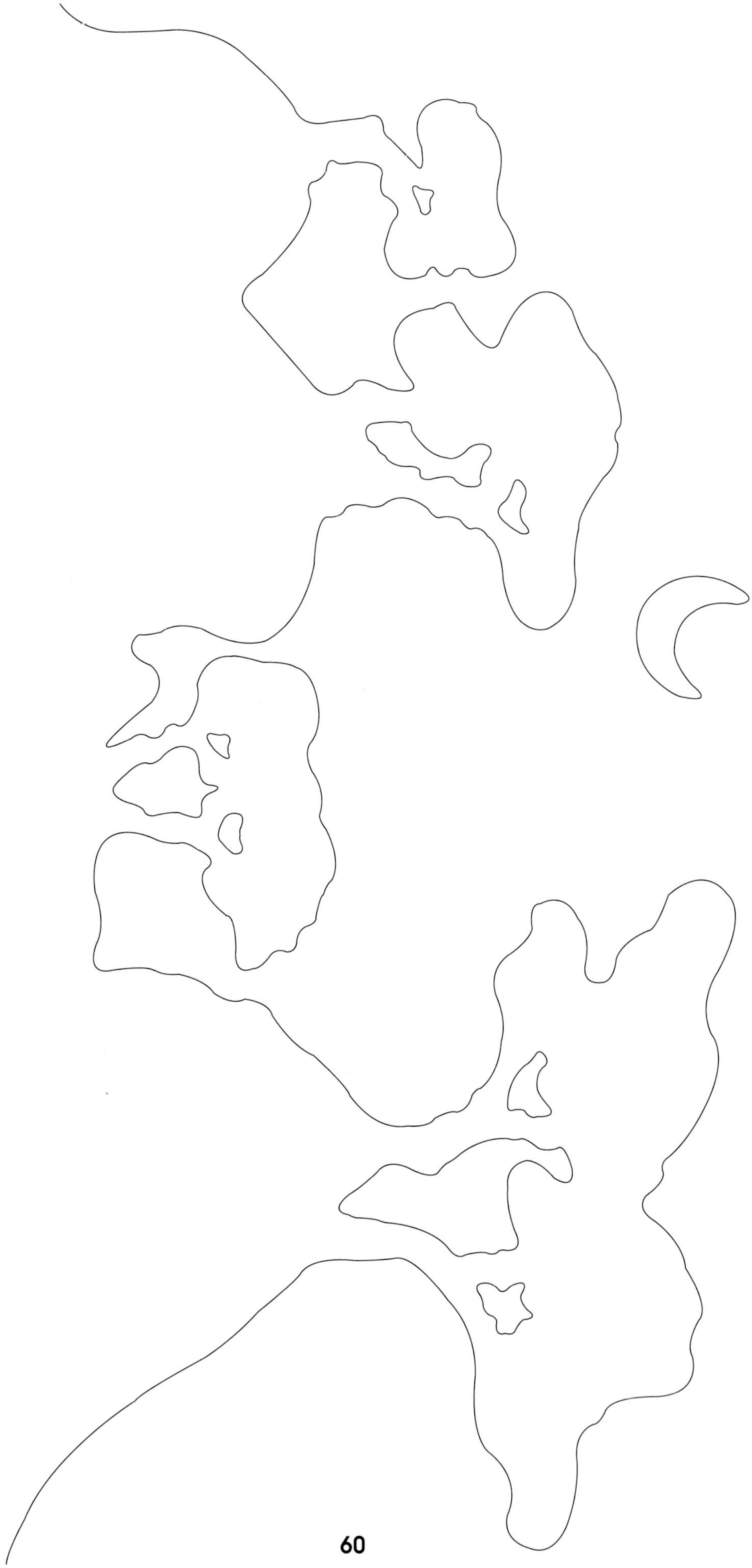

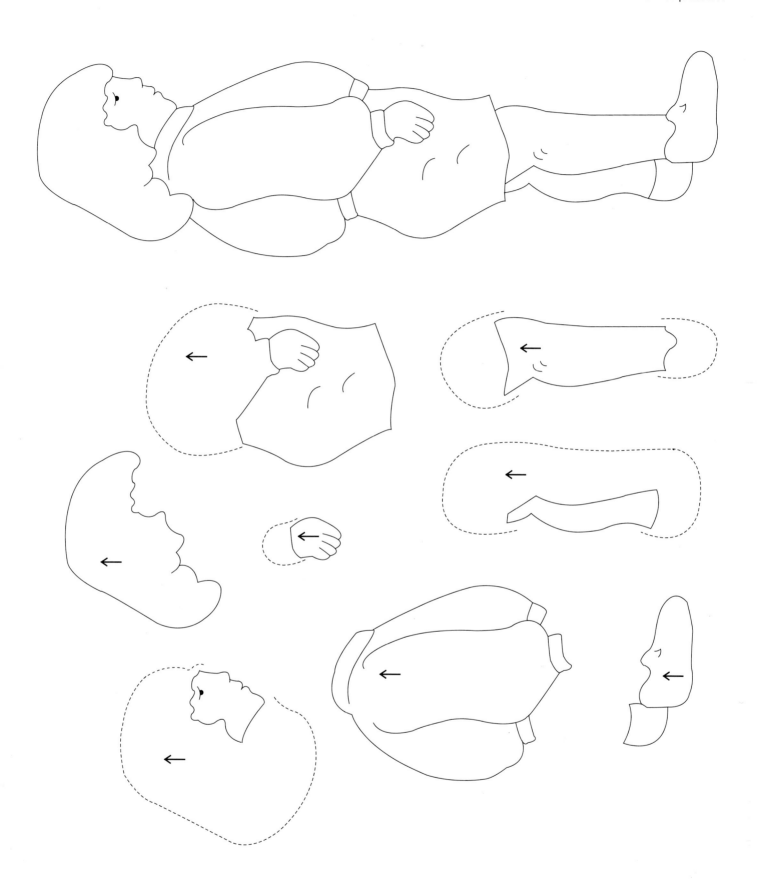

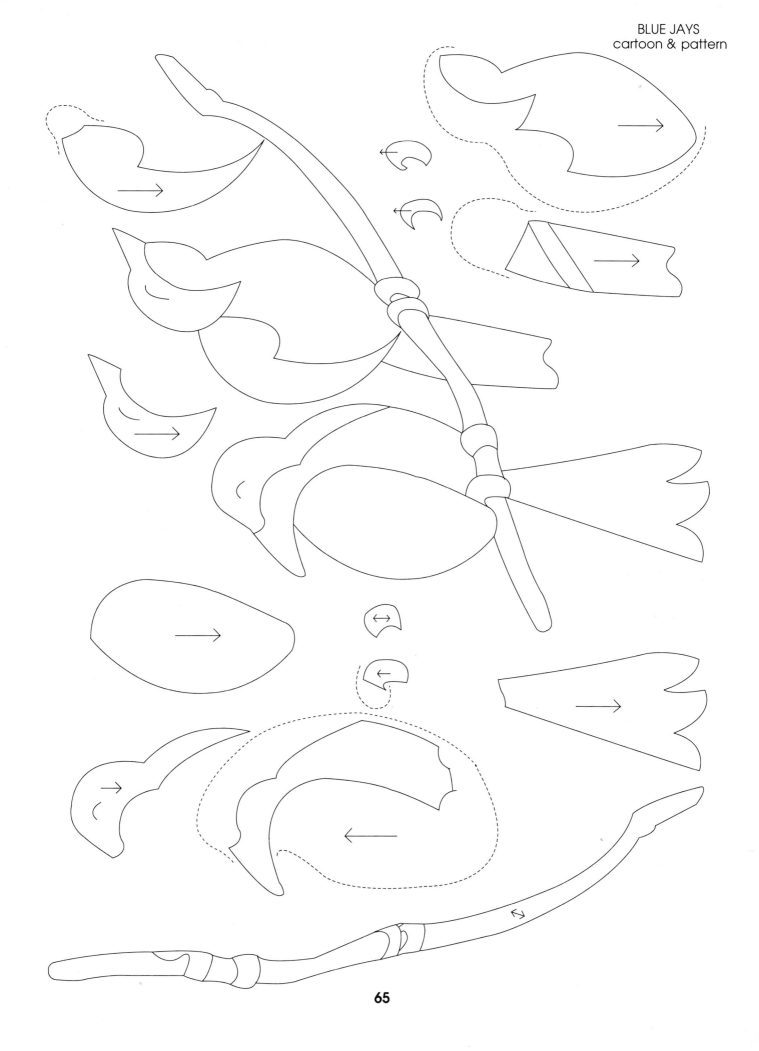

65

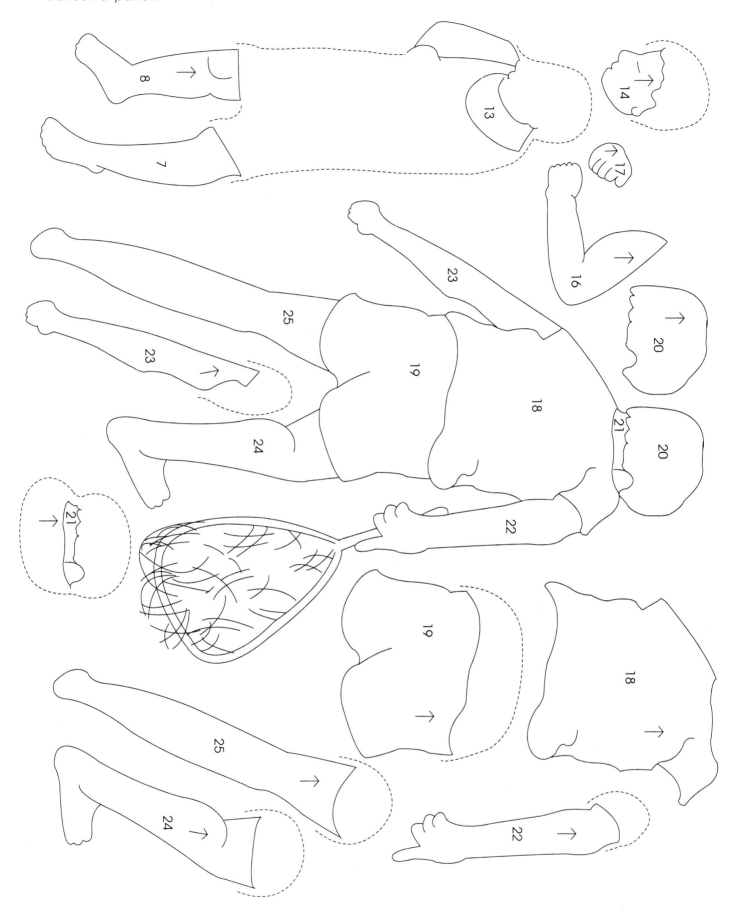

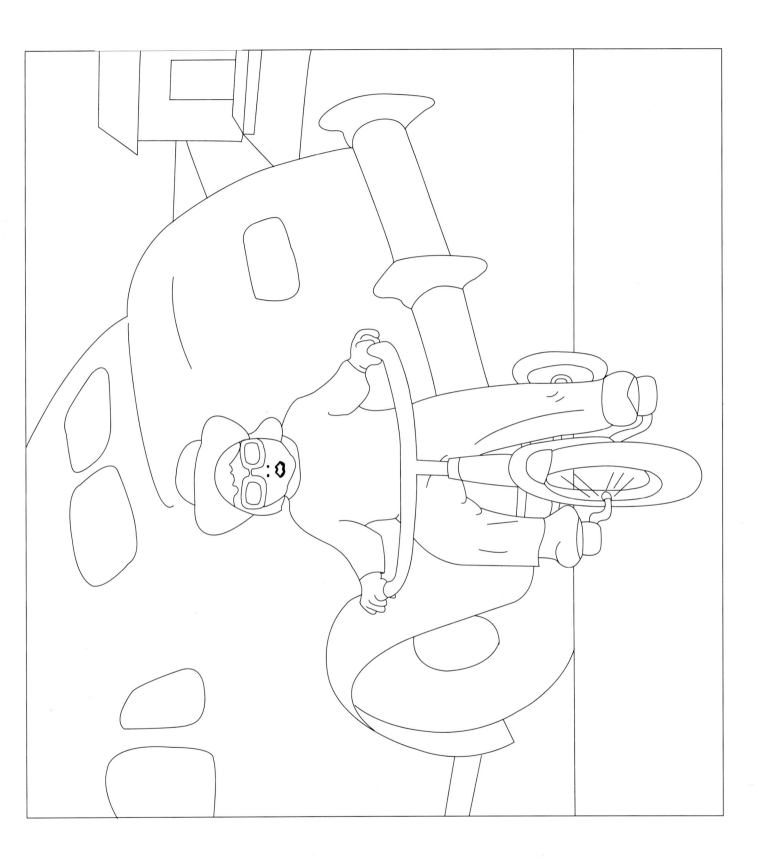

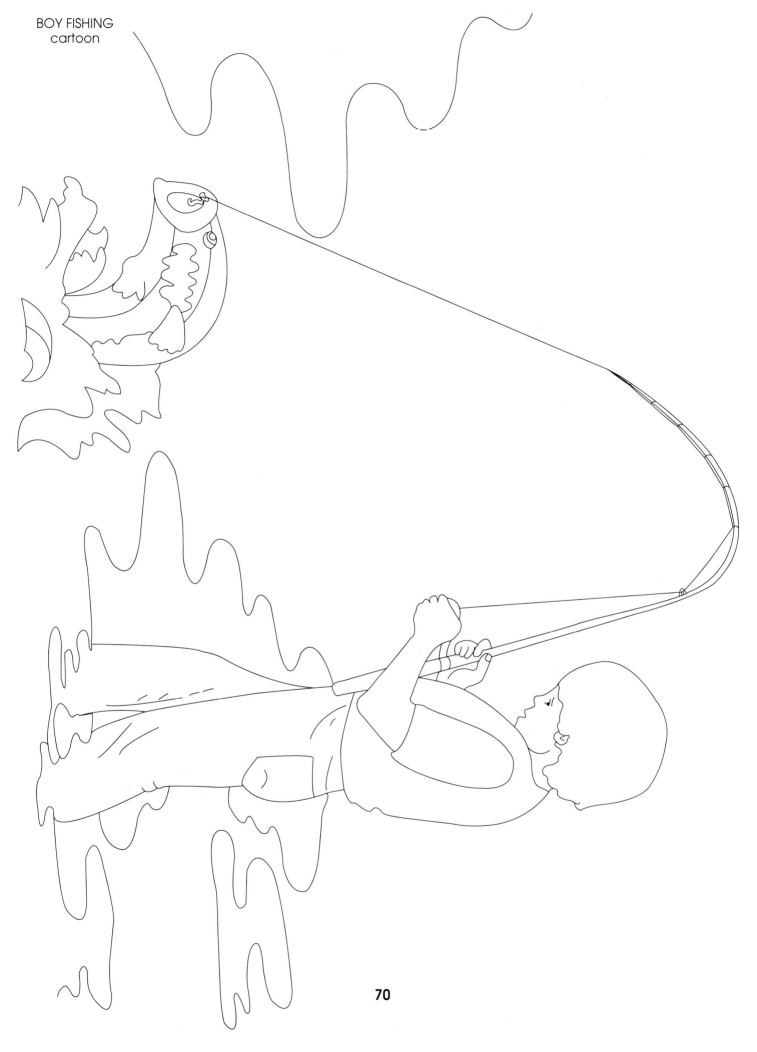

Hang Glider Over Yosemite, 71" x 76", 1989.

And Crown Her Good With Brotherhood, 72" x 72", 1986.

Above:
Baseball Batter panel from *And Crown Her Good With Brotherhood.*

Below Right:
Polliwog Collectors panel from *And Crown Her Good With Brotherhood.*

Boy Fishing panel from *And Crown Her Good With Brotherhood*. See page 70 for the cartoon.

take his or her original home the same day. Dorophoto is located at 1253 Springfield Ave.; the phone number is (908) 464-4598.

The society is also looking for photos from the early 1900s to present — of town events, stores, class activities, schools, athletic teams (P.A.L., adult, school), civic groups, places of worship, early automobiles, roadways, older homes, buildings, fire, rescue, and

during the week - Sen... station with

Fabric center invites public

Krupnick Bros. Inc. at 909 Rahway Avenue, Union, is a wholesale distributor of decorative residential and contract fabrics that has been catering to the design trades since 1924.

It sells through 24 regional "to the trade" showrooms including the New York Design Center at 200 Lexington Avenue, the D.C.O.T.A. Center, Dania, Fla., and the Pacific Design Center, Los Angeles.

To help dispose of inventory of discontinued patterns

its Union warehouse to the public for the first time in 60 years—for close outs only. The showroom will be closed during sale hours.

Real savings of 75 per cent from original retail prices will be offered on domestic and imported upholstery, drapery and printed fabrics. Most were available through interior designers only.

Sale dates and times are September 23 to October 4 from 5 to 9 p.m. and October 5 and 6, noon to

And Crown Her Good With Brotherhood, Boy Fishing Panel. (Detail).

Hummingbird, 12" x 9", 1989.
Cotton appliqué with embroidery; basted for quilting.
See page 64 for the cartoon and pattern.

And Crown Her Good With Brotherhood, Boy Fishing
Panel. (Detail).

Grandmother panel from *And Crown Her Good With Brotherhood.*

Scrambling the Tors of Ve Da Wu, 54" x 72", 1989 (appliquéd top before quilting).

At the Window, 10" x 11¼", 1989. Appliquéd cat is velvet. See page 68 for the cartoon.

Lift Off Miniature, 10" x 9", 1987. See page 61 for the pattern of the girl standing in the center panel.

Benny and the Brontosaurus, 9½" x 9", 1987. See page 57 for the pattern.

The Thrill, 14" x 13", 1988. See page 42 for the instructions.

Boy On Tricycle, 12" x 12", 1989. See page 69 for the cartoon.

Aurora Borealis, 45" x 36", 1985. (Detail).

Scrub Jays, 9½" x 13", 1989. See page 65 for the cartoon and pattern.

Fuchsia Blossoms, 14" x 10½", 1989. (Detail) See page 27 for the instructions and pages 58-59 for the cartoon and pattern.

Silhouette – Trees, appliquéd yoke on a shirt, 15" x 9", 1981. (Detail) See page 60 for the cartoon.

~ American Quilter's Society ~

dedicated to publishing books
for today's quilters

The following AQS publications are currently available:

American Beauties: Rose & Tulip Quilts
by Gwen Marston & Joe Cunningham
#1907: AQS, 1988, 96 pages, softbound, $14.95

America's Pictorial Quilts by Caron L. Mosey
#1662: AQS, 1985, 112 pages, hardbound, $19.95

Applique Designs: My Mother Taught Me to Sew
by Faye Anderson
#2121: AQS, 1990, 80 pages, softbound, $12.95

Arkansas Quilts: Arkansas Warmth
Arkansas Quilter's Guild, Inc.
#1908: AQS, 1987, 144 pages, hardbound, $24.95

The Art of Hand Appliqué by Laura Lee Fritz
#2122: AQS, 1990, 80 pages, softbound, $14.95

...Ask Helen More About Quilting Designs by Helen Squire
#2099: AQS, 1990, 54 pages, 17x11, spiral-bound, $14.95

Collection of Favorite Quilts, A by Judy Florence
#2119 AQS, 1990, 136 pages, softbound, $18.95

Dear Helen, Can You Tell Me? ...all about quilting designs
by Helen Squire
#1820: AQS, 1987, 56 pages, 17 x 11, spiral-bound, $12.95

Dyeing & Overdyeing of Cotton Fabrics by Judy Mercer Tescher
#2030: AQS, 1990, 54 pages, softbound, $9.95

Fun & Fancy Machine Quiltmaking by Lois Smith
#1982: AQS, 1989, 144 pages, softbound, $19.95

Gallery of American Quilts: 1849-1988
#1938: AQS, 1988, 128 pages, softbound, $19.95

Gallery of American Quilts 1860-1989: Book II
#2129: AQS, 1990, 128 pages, softbound, $19.95

The Grand Finale: A Quilter's Guide to Finishing Projects
by Linda Denner
#1924: AQS, 1988, 96 pages, softbound, $14.95

Heirloom Miniatures by Tina M. Gravatt
#2097: AQS, 1990, 64 pages, softbound, $9.95

Home Study Course in Quiltmaking by Jeannie M. Spears
#2031: AQS, 1990, 240 pages, softbound, $19.95

The Ins and Outs: Perfecting the Quilting Stitch
by Patricia J. Morris
#2120: AQS, 1990, 96 pages, softbound, $9.95

Irish Chain Quilts: A Workbook of Irish Chains & Related Patterns by Joyce B. Peaden
#1906: AQS, 1988, 96 pages, softbound, $14.95

Missouri Heritage Quilts by Bettina Havig
#1718: AQS, 1986, 104 pages, softbound, $14.95

Nancy Crow: Quilts and Influences by Nancy Crow
#1981: AQS, 1990, 256 pages, hardcover, $29.95

No Dragons on My Quilt by Jean Ray Laury with
Ritva Laury and Lizabeth Laury
#2153: AQS, 1990, 52 pages, hardcover, $12.95

Oklahoma Heritage Quilts
Oklahoma Quilt Heritage Project
#2032: AQS, 1990, 144 pages, softbound, $19.95

Scarlet Ribbons: American Indian Technique for Today's Quilters by Helen Kelley
#1819: AQS, 1987, 104 pages, softbound, $15.95

Sets & Borders by Gwen Marston and Joe Cunningham
#1821: AQS, 1987, 104 pages, softbound, $14.95

Somewhere in Between: Quilts and Quilters of Illinois
by Rita Barrow Barber
#1790: AQS, 1986, 78 pages, softbound, $14.95

Stenciled Quilts for Christmas by Marie Monteith Sturmer
#2098: AQS, 1990, 104 pages, softbound, $14.95

Texas Quilts–Texas Treasures
Texas Heritage Quilt Society
#1760: AQS, 1986, 160 pages, hardbound, $24.95

Treasury of Quilting Designs, A by Linda Goodmon Emery
#2029: AQS, 1990, 80 pages, 14"x11", spiral-bound, $14.95

These books can be found in local bookstores and quilt shops. If you are unable to locate a title in your area, you can order by mail from AQS, P.O. Box 3290, Paducah, KY 42002-3290. Please add $1 for the first book and 40¢ for each additional one to cover postage and handling.